ENTREPRENEURSHIP?
KINGDOM BUILDING KEYS

Dr. Rae Pearson
"E-DIVA"

ISBN: 1-4196-7439-0
ISBN-13: 9781419674396
Library of Congress Control Number: 2007905641

Visit www.booksurge.com to order additional copies.

Contents

Dedication

I would like to thank my mother and father for giving me their entrepreneurial spirit and for their assistance in my early years, both of which helped me grow into the person I am today. I would also like to thank my current staff.

Without the trainees and mentors (many of whom are current and former CEOs of corporations), former employers and current employees(for motivation) and the volume of other entrepreneurs I interviewed, this book would not have been possible. It would be impossible to name everyone, but I thank you all.

At the top of the list of people who inspired me are my children; my sister Sheila; my spiritual leader, Apostle Dr. Oscar J. Underwood; and my Cathedral of Praise Ministries & Church International family.

But above all else, God is the head of my life.

About the Author

Dr. Rae Pearson is also known as the Entrpreneur and Employment Diva (or E-Diva). She has worked extensively as an executive recruiter, small business trainer, career coach, employment expert and radio personality for 27 years. Dr. Pearson holds an Honorary Doctorate Degree In Humanities.

Dr. Rae Pearson wrote this book for the people who are struggling with their purpose of building wealth as a business owner. After over 20 years of running a multi-million dollar Personnel Staffing and Training business in a Midwest Town coupled with many years of counseling entrepreneurs and co-authoring the grant to start one of the Midwest's first Women Business Enterprise Centers; the questions and solutions made this book an easy feat. The book consists of many entrepreneurs asking questions and Dr. Pearson (E-Diva) sharing some of her ups and downs; But God!

"If you have never had a business or ran a business it's hard to give advice without experience." said Dr. Pearson dubbed as the E-Diva who can talk the talk and walk the walk. One of her pet peeves is the bad actors and actresses that give business ownership a bad name in our society. And the Entrepreneurship Centers that are popping up everywhere that don't have business owners as managers to direct a new person seeking help with the right guidance.

 Kingdom Building Keys is meant to inspire anyone who has a hearts desire to be a team-building economic guru (A Business Owner). This is the beginning of a series of books to help God's kingdom grow. Bishop T.D. Jakes, Apostle Dr. Oscar J. Underwood, John Maxwell, and Dr. Charles Stanley, Joyce Meyers to name a few are great teachers that I have studied and believe that are clearly in touch with kingdom building. We all have purpose and after reading this book I hope you have a clearer picture about whether working as an entrepreneur or working as a strong team member is your destiny; which is your rightful choice.

Hats off to all the nations entrepreneurs', it's a hard job; but someone has to do it!

I'd like to Thank God for the patience in writing this book and spreading this wisdom of Kingdom Building Keys.

Foreword

It has been said that people who look are common, but people who can see are rare. The world is full of those who sit on the sideline watching and wondering what has happened and why better did not happen for them. However, those who are the catalysts in life simply dream and envision better, then set their course to bring it about. The greatest opportunities will always end up in the hands of those whose vision cause them to dare to go beyond the limits in their own previous experiences, understanding that wise effort will always be rewarded.

In His faithfulness, God places points of light in every generation to illuminate the path of humanity so that personal dreams and aspirations can meet up with personal achievement and success. He elevates proven leaders above the crowd so that they might teach others how to connect with their own potential and life possibilities. Such a person is Dr. Rae Pearson, whose life is the personification of the empowerment that causes impossible dreams to come true when one chooses to live life and conduct business by the principles of the Word of God. She is living proof that the true advantage in life comes from purposeful living based on Biblical standards that makes it possible to embrace the best that one can be.

In this book, Dr. Rae Pearson dares to reveal to the world the secret to her amazing personal success that transformed her life and her business success. Her story is one that anyone who is serious about getting the best out of life truly needs to read. Excellence without apologies by systematically following Biblical principles has been her life coach, which has caused her to leave a legacy of empowerment and a path of essence for millions who have been waiting for God to send them the answers that they need. Their lives will be immeasurably transformed by applying the principles that Dr. Pearson shares.

No one who dares to read this book with a hunger and thirst for the manifestation of their own dreams and potential, will ever be denied a better life. There is no way that anyone who truly listens to her life lessons with an open heart will ever again find themselves willing to accept mediocrity when God has destined them to be so much more. Resources are available in abundance for those who know who they are and understand their mission. Dr. Rae is living proof in every sense of the word. It is my prayer that after reading her story, millions will take up the challenge to advance into God's best that He wants them to live. This is their season - this is their time; a "Rae" of light has entered to curse their darkness. The path is now visible - the path is now clear.

Wishing you the life you were meant to live,

Dr. Oscar J. Underwood, Jr.
Apostle to the Marketplace
September 20, 2007

Introduction

One of my favorite modern parables tells the story of a conversation between God and a woman seeking guidance because she feels beaten down by life.

"What should I do?" asks the woman.

"Build a better world," said God.

"But how?" she cries, since she already feels defeated. "The world is such a vast and complicated place, and I am small and useless. What can I possibly do?"

God, in all His wisdom, said, "Just build a better you."

What does this story have to do with launching your own successful business, you might ask?

Everything!

The power of transformation lies in your hands.

Do you dream about building a business of your own? You're not alone. A U.S. Labor Department study shows that 70% of Americans over the age of 21 want to start their own business.

Or are you looking for a better job? Wondering how to stand up for your rights at work?

Well, you've come to exactly the right place.

Believe me, I know how easy it can be to get discouraged. But I'm living proof that if you take the right steps you can and will succeed.

That's what this book is about. I've put together the most helpful, informative and motivating tips I know of about work and business so you can get the job you want or open the business of your dreams. Tips that will help you learn how to work best with bosses and co-workers or manage a loyal, skilled staff.

Over the last 20 years or so, I've enjoyed an incredible career. I've joined the ranks of a small percentage of successful Midwestern black women entrepreneurs and have achieved many honors, including my status as a Certified Personnel Consultant and being the proud owner of an award-winning independent executive recruiting and staffing firm.

As a management consultant, I've assisted Fortune 500 corporations nationwide, providing them with top-notch staffing and training. I'm a member of the Governor's Commission on Minority and Women's Business Enterprises. I'm an expert employment advisor and have been called upon to act as an expert witness in the courts. As a career coach and entrepreneurial trainer, I founded my own entrepreneur program in the 1990's before assisting a not –for- profit in getting a grant for a program in 2000.

I've been a talk-show radio host, answering questions from callers about starting and running their own businesses. I've helped entrepreneurs through an online employment and training site under the cyber name "E-Diva" (the "E" stands for entrepreneur, education and excellence).

I'd like to help you, too. This book is meant to be a guide; to help you achieve an edge and live up to your greatest professional and personal potential. The advice in this book stems in part from real- life problems and questions I've been asked as E-Diva over the years; I'll also cover subjects such as how to avoid costly (but common) mistakes, the importance of selecting a good company name, how to avoid a sexist banker, how to find accountants or attorneys and how to hire loyal, skilled staff members.

I'll also share my personal stories and let you in on some hard-won secrets and concrete advice. Many women and minority individuals are struggling to open businesses, but racism and sexism can prove to be frustrating barriers to their success.

But they don't have to be. Because no matter who you are, there are specific steps you can take (and pitfalls to avoid) to achieve unbelievable success.

I should know, because that's exactly what I did.

THE E-DIVA STORY

My story began many years ago when, as a small-town African-American girl from Indiana, I dared to have big dreams. I owe much of my optimism and fortitude to my parents, who were the wind beneath my wings, always encouraging my creativity within the arts, my education, and my business career. I wasn't exactly sure what I'd do for my life's work, but I figured I had to start somewhere.

I'll tell you this, no one was more optimistic!

I've enjoyed several careers. I've been a singer, blueprint operator, dental assistant, popcorn maker, housewife, manager of a temporary service, executive recruiter, and last but not least, a business owner. I loved singing, but a life of suitcases and constant travel took its toll. When I became a mother, I made the conscious decision that I didn't want to be out on the road singing with a child.

So I ran through my other options. I loved music but I didn't want to teach it. I had aspirations to running my own business. But where would I start? How could I establish myself without any experience?

You know that old saying about one door closing and another opening? That's what happened. At the time, I ran a small, home-based business selling Avon products, and discovered I was really good at it.

Then one day, there was a knock at my door.

It was a man who happened to be friends with the owner of an employment agency. He had noticed my business acumen, and thought his friend would be interested in meeting me. So he arranged for an interview. Long story short, I landed my first job in the employment services business.

Here I was, a singer still holding onto fantasies of being discovered in show business, when I would get discovered … but in the employment business instead.

After working for that staffing firm in Chicago, Illinois for two years, I moved back to my home town in Indiana. I transferred the skills I'd developed to another employment agency, and by then, I knew I had found my calling. I can think of no greater thrill than to perfectly match an employer and employee or to help another person discover their lifelong passion, as I have.

Eureka!

THE BIRTH OF ALPHA RAE

The story is a simple one: While working for someone else had its benefits, I felt compelled to go out on my own. So one day in 1980 I decided to make it happen.

My then-spouse assisted me in getting a $5,000 bank loan, and step-by-step I built a profitable business for myself and my family.

The first and most important move I made was finding an appropriate location (location, location, location!) for my business, but naming my business came in at a close second. I chose a name that held special meaning for me: Alpha Rae Personnel Inc. To begin with, this was my first employment service, and "alpha" means first or beginning; Rae is my first name. I also remembered that alpha rays are positive rays from the sun.

The name took. Sales took off. Before I knew it, I was bringing in over $5,000 a week.

In the beginning, I specialized Alpha Rae's services, focusing on finding employment for temporary workers in light industrial and clerical fields. But we quickly grew, and it wasn't long before I expanded into executive searches for a number of Fortune 500 companies (including Bristol Meyers, Brown & Williamson, Lincoln Life Insurance Company, Raytheon, ITT Aerospace, and International Truck & Engine Corporation).

Unbelievable!

By 1985, I saw a need to branch out into training, mainly to provide programs for those who came in to test for jobs but were ill-prepared for the workforce.

Then came our big break.

We won an Indiana state contract under what was then the new (now old) Job Training Partnership Act. This led to several larger training contracts in the private sector. From there, we naturally moved into training for today's small business economy with entrepreneurship training and training for the self-employed.

In 1986, I was in the midst of a divorce.

I also made two million dollars.

What an experience to be happy and sad at the same time! With glowing referrals, Alpha Rae grew larger and larger. One day, we received a telephone call from a company in Indianapolis (who had heard about us from a happy client). We grew larger still.

With a proven record of excellence (I'll talk about the importance of reputation and testimonials in later chapters), we were awarded a $2.5 million prime contract for an Indianapolis manufacturing company, which, of course, afforded Alpha Rae the opportunity to open its Indianapolis location. Today, we have expanded into 20 other states, working everywhere with teaming agreements and contracts nationwide, and Alpha Rae's sales reach into the millions.

BEHIND THE SCENES: GETTING INTO AND OUT OF TROUBLE SPOTS IN BUSINESS

While I've enjoyed tremendous success after starting with only a modest bank loan, I've also hit a few obstacles along the way. I want you to understand success never comes easily, and that it truly pays to do your homework. Here are a few roadblocks that I faced:

- **We needed more money (and fast) in order to grow.** Growth for us had been rapid, so finding money sources had always been an issue for my company, as it is for other small businesses in the same situation. It wasn't easy to learn how to handle cash flow issues.
- **We needed experienced personnel.** I believe in excellence, so I needed to find employees who understood that quality and customer service determine the leading winners in business — and that all employees would have to deliver.
- **We needed global exposure in a small town.** As a woman and minority business owner, I wanted to think big … and brainstormed routes of expansion early on.

A CAUTIONARY TALE

As new business owner, I met many good, helpful people. But I'm also sorry to say I met the kind of greedy business people you never want to know.

Here's one sad tale about a downright predatory lending firm.

As we grew financially, we couldn't find anyone in my small hometown with the foresight to understand our potential. I really believe my gender and color were deal breakers back then, so without a husband or man to sign or co-sign on a loan, I quickly surmised it probably wasn't going to happen.

Consequently, I had to keep Alpha Rae's overhead to a minimum, actually turning down opportunities.

Then a Wisconsin-based company called with a plan to relieve us of all our back-office headaches. They would take over our invoicing and collections. They would advance my weekly payroll cost while cash flowed in from our big contracts.

All right! It seemed like a dream come true.

Unfortunately, it turned out to be a nightmare.

For a good long run, it did work.

Until I figured out what was really happening.

At first, the commission checks I received seemed like "found money." But the money we obtained from this Wisconsin firm was increasingly inconsistent with our sales, so we decided to discontinue the service and to handle our own accounts.

I only wish it had been that easy.

When I notified the lending company (with my lawyer present) that we would be terminating their contract, I learned the real meaning of "predatory." Our dealings got very ugly, very legally complicated, cost a fortune and almost put me out of business (by the way, this debacle occurred in 1999, so it just goes to show that even seasoned business professionals can still learn lessons).

Remember the lesson about being unevenly yoked to the wrong mate if you're married? Well, the same holds true in your business relationships. Take it from me, you really need to know exactly with whom you are getting involved. I found out the hard way the importance of doing your homework, asking the impolite questions and never, ever assuming. I've also learned that women- and minority-owned businesses are particularly susceptible to this pitfall, and remain vulnerable to many other predatory practices because we often struggle to access traditional loans. I've learned not to do big business with strangers.

Finally, I've learned from experience that if it seems to be too good to be true, it probably is.

IN A NUTSHELL: DR. RAE PEARSON'S TIPS FOR BUSINESS SUCCESS

When people ask me what the trick is to succeeding, I tell them that there are certain keys to everlasting success in business — but no tricks!

My tried and true keys are:

- **Location, location, location.** What's true in the real estate market is true for business owners. Where you physically locate your business can play a part in determining your company's success – or failure.
- **A good company name.** Branding in the 21st century business world is critical. Choose a name for your business that reflects what you do and how well you do it.
- **Choose the right bank.** A bank and banker who understand you are imperative. In some ways, nothing can be more important to the success of your business than the

financial institution you use to support your dream. This applies to hiring an attorney and accountant, too. Investigate them as they investigate you.

- **Hire a loyal staff.** Who you have working for you is obviously a key factor in your business. Carefully choose your employees, looking for professional people with vision who want to grow with you.
- **Pay attention.** You might think it goes without saying, but many businesses fail because the owner begins to take things for granted. Review all details of your business … every day.
- **Do strategic planning.** A vital component to all successful businesses, strategic planning should be done on a daily, weekly, monthly and yearly basis.
- **Adapt to change.** Being flexible and able to readjust to a changing business landscape is vital to succeeding in today's business world. Reevaluate as needed for effective management.
- **Value associates and mentors.** In the world of business, the old adage "what goes around comes around" rings true. Be respectful not only of those with whom you work, but with all those who surround you in your professional life.
- **Sign all your company checks.** Do not use commercially made signature stamps. They are a surefire way to get into trouble, as they are just too easily abused.
- **Deliver excellent customer service.** Nothing is more important than the way you treat your customers. While all business owners realize they are dependant on their customers, they too often neglect to direct sufficient resources toward providing superior customer service.

WORDS OF WISDOM

Finally, I believe the best work lessons can be found in Proverbs 3:5 in The Good Book.

"Lean not on your own understanding, but in all thy ways, acknowledge Him."

God provides me with wonderful opportunities to learn from my failures, and I strive to acknowledge Him in my successes every day of my life. While I am by no means perfect, I understand I am a work in progress, and that it is up to me to improve both myself and the world around me.

Remember, only you can build a better you! That means you can build a satisfying, successful professional and personal life – starting today. I hope this book helps you on that path.

Chapter One

Are You An Entrepreneur?

" Before you agree to do anything that might add even the smallest amount of stress to your life, ask yourself: What is my truest intention? Give yourself time to let a 'yes' resound within you. When it's right, I guarantee that your entire body will feel it."
—Oprah Winfrey

Everyone has their own "A-Ha!" moment as an entrepreneur.

You know, that moment of crystal clarity when it hits you: You're destined to call your own shots and stop taking orders from people you don't respect.

My "A-Ha!" moment happened in the early years of forming my employee recruitment company. It was beginning to dawn on me that my "partner" expected me to do all the heavy lifting. I was hiring employees, overseeing the books, managing the office … you name it.

One day when my "partner" asked me to take on one more task, I realized he was getting a much better part of the deal.

The next day I was on my own, running around town looking for office space for my own employee recruitment company.

But that's the entrepreneur's mindset, distilled into its purest form. We want to lead the pack, not take orders from people destined to be in the back of the pack.

After all, when the Marines hit the beach at Normandy, someone had to jump off the boat first.

History is strewn with beach-jumpers. Or in our case, people who want to work for themselves. Look at David Packard, founder of Hewlett-Packard. He once said he didn't want to start his company to make a lot of money. He just wanted to be his own boss, but since he worked for General Electric that wasn't going to happen.

Then there's John H. Johnson, the founder of *Jet* magazine. He created *Jet* on November 1, 1951, to celebrate the lives of African Americans after realizing there wasn't anything else like it out in the magazine marketplace. So he filled the void.

IS IT FOR YOU?

Both Packard and Johnson adhered to the classic entrepreneurial theory, which is summarized well by something William Shakespeare wrote: "To thine own self be true."

This seemingly abstract philosophy is crucial for anyone thinking about starting a new business.

So let's start with a tough question: Is starting a new business right for you? Because the hard truth is, entrepreneurship is not for everyone. Knowing your strengths (and weaknesses) is the secret to success, whether you are starting your own business or navigating your professional growth as an employee within a company. Timing is also important. Launching a new enterprise might not be right for you right now due to circumstances.

On the other hand, if you're struggling to fit gigantic dreams into a tiny cubicle or your initiative is being squashed repeatedly where you work, now's the time to start sketching out your trustworthy (and essential) roadmap for your future goals.

You wouldn't try to get somewhere new before you looked up directions, would you?

Your roadmap should include all the elements of any good business plan: Product descriptions, marketing analysis, target audience, financials, even your personal situation all must be considered in depth. Once you decide to plunge ahead, I recommend networking right away.

> **FAST FACT:**
> **Did you know that only 30% of business start-ups actually survive longer than five years?**

It is very important to do your homework and conduct a difficult self-examination before you invest your house and family funds on a business venture that might not suit your personality or fit your situation. That's what this chapter will help you gauge.

First and foremost, you must explore your motivations. Write down the reasons why you want to launch a new business (you can turn back to these reasons during the harder times to remind yourself exactly why the long hours and great personal risk are, in the end, highly rewarding).

If you are only out to make money but lack enthusiasm about the work behind the business, well now, that's a red flag.

On the other hand, maybe you can't stop thinking about how you would build up your markets, or why your products and services are important in the larger scheme of things. Do you wake up wondering how you would pitch your product to a new customer?

That's a good sign.

As I mentioned before, my personal "A-Ha!" moment occurred during a time when I was working for someone who said they wanted me as their partner.

Well, sort of.

I quickly realized what my prospective "partner" really wanted was a worker. You get the picture. I would be doing all the work and he would be sitting across the office reading the paper. I didn't want to do that.

I'm not against hard work. Having extensive experience in a franchise, I was well versed in long hours. But I also knew when people were trying to take advantage of me. So I saw him coming a mile away.

Here I was, carrying the barbells, doing all the work, but not getting rewarded appropriately in return. I did everything from contacting customers to checking receivables by myself. So I thought to myself, "if I can do it all for him, why not do it all for myself … in name as well as in deed?"

At the time my now-former husband worked at a bank. He assisted me in securing a $5,000 loan to get me started, and then I was up and running. I followed no particular business Bible or mentor. Instead, I learned as I went along.

But I did seek a little bit of practical advice.

I had a girlfriend who told me about a class that was being taught on running a business. I signed up.

The class covered topics like margins and markup, and the other essential nuts and bolts information about running your own show. It ran for eight weeks and I took it twice. It was too technical, and most of the information was over my head. I knew I needed a more remedial approach.

After the class, I began walking up and down the streets of Fort Wayne, Indiana looking for office space. I must admit, this is one instance where I dove in headfirst. Perhaps I should have thought about it. But as it turned out, acting quickly worked in my favor.

I consider this one of the eternal balancing acts of the true entrepreneur: While you must always do your homework, don't ever doubt your instincts. Few books can prepare you for making a last-minute major decision. And remember, if you're the boss, those decisions will always rest in your hands.

WHAT MAKES A GOOD ENTREPRENEUR?

As I said, not everyone should start a new business. If you can't bring yourself to get out of bed in the morning and you're seeking an easy ride, you might want to think again. Personal drive is an essential trait for the successful entrepreneur.

Launching your own business requires a great deal of drive and tenacity. Think about

THE E-DIVA'S FIVE "E'S" OF ENTREPRENEURIAL SUCCESS

Through the years, I've developed a code I call my "Five E's". If I adhere to the code, and to the Five E's, I know I'm always on the right track. If you can apply these Five E's to your professional endeavors, they can work for you, too. To paraphrase the old American Express commercial, "don't leave home without them."

• **Enthusiasm.** Ralph Waldo Emerson said, "Nothing great is ever achieved without enthusiasm." It's hard to argue with that. If you don't love what you do, what's the point? Life is short. Do what you love and sort the rest out later.

• **Education.** Do your homework. More businesses fail because entrepreneurs are surprised by events they didn't expect – like the ski resort owner who didn't see global warming coming or the horse-and-buggy proprietor in 1903 who didn't see Henry Ford coming, you don't want to be blind-sided by events that could take down your business.

• **Economics.** Money dominates the culture of any start-up, so you might as well get used to it. Getting a grip on financing and cash flow now can save you a lot of headaches down the line. Start by creating a financing plan and a budget and work up from there.

• **Employees.** Never underestimate the value of the people you hire. As Henry Ford once said, "You can take my factories, burn up my buildings, but give me my people and I'll build the business right back up again." In other words, you are going nowhere as a business owner without good people you can depend on.

• **Ethics.** Always practice good ethics. I remember going to an auto mechanic who told me the repairs on my car could be $150 – a previous mechanic had said $500. The first mechanic had practiced good ethics and, as a result, is my mechanic for life.

it this way: All of a sudden you will gain an incredible amount of control and flexibility over your schedule.

Depending on who you are, this can be a good or bad thing. If you really want to cancel all your meetings and take the day off, you can. However, you won't get paid if you don't work, so too many days out fishing might lead you right out of business.

It's equally important to be someone who stubbornly perseveres. That means not getting discouraged too easily and wearing a smile for your clients, even in the worst of circumstances.

Believe it or not, research has shown that many entrepreneurs were actually not high achievers in school.

One study conducted by Northwestern Mutual Life found some interesting character tendencies of entrepreneurs and used their findings to create a quiz measuring a person's Entrepreneur Quotient (EQ). Factors included family background (the children of immigrants often scored high), tendency to be stubborn as children (most successful business owners must have taxed their parents horribly), and even enjoyment of group activities (you weren't likely to find most successful entrepreneurs on the tennis team or in the chess – or any other – club at school).

Often, business owners thrive on competition but are equally driven by an intense passion for their field. Usually they are natural leaders, but in my view, to be really successful it's also important to know when to take advice. And perhaps most importantly, entrepreneurs often welcome (calculated!) risk-taking of all shapes and sizes.

This leads me to risk-taking.

There's really no way around it when you decide to call yourself boss. Not even your paycheck is guaranteed.

However, I'm not talking about a reckless gamble when I speak of risk. What I mean is that after you conduct scrupulous research, seek appropriate consultation and carry out extensive outreach, decisions (which are never an exact science) must be made. This aspect of entrepreneurship deserves some thought, particularly if uncertainty upsets you. In the best scenario, you will be faced with uncertainty often. The fact is many entrepreneurs enjoy an element of risk in their lives.

Other common traits of a good entrepreneur include patience and flexibility. In all probability, your profits will not be soaring after a week in business. It will be necessary to keep the faith and remain consistently proactive, while always realistically assessing your business situation. Remember, everything worthwhile takes time and effort.

And speaking of time, are you willing (and able) to work until 1 a.m. to get the job done? Or to fly out to see a client in Ohio at their last minute request?

All that said, no hard and fast rules define the character of successful entrepreneurs. The main secret lies in your own enthusiasm for your business and your tireless devotion to the work itself.

You'll need to be honest with yourself and your family about what it really takes to launch a successful business. You'll want to look at your personal budget, sit down with your family and discuss any and all concerns. Did you recently have a baby? Did your spouse recently lose his or her job? Timing should never be dismissed when starting a new business.

There are two sides to every coin, and business ownership is no exception. What's attractive to one person might prove wholly distasteful to another, so again, it's important to be realistic about who you are as you weigh the pros and cons of starting your own business.

THE BENEFITS

- **You're the boss.** You will no longer need to ask permission for things or get sign-off on a brochure promoting your new product. The buck stops with you. That means you sign all the checks! Do you enjoy exerting firm, confident decisions?

- **There's room for creativity.** Remember all those meetings where you had to bite your tongue? When you felt your frustration rising as every new (good!) idea was immediately squelched due to rigid corporate groupthink? Not anymore. You can experiment with each and every new idea to your heart's content. The only caveat here is that it helps to stay focused.

- **Flexibility.** While large corporations often benefit from large marketing budgets and pervasive distribution, smaller companies wield a distinct advantage in their ability to make swift decisions. Did you notice a low return on your web advertising campaign? You (without any office politics) can change it overnight.

- **You'll be making your own money (and perhaps much more of it).** Many people choose to go into business for themselves because they tire of making large profits for their companies rather than reaping the rewards themselves. And the fact is, starting your own business can lead you to far higher income levels than you would achieve as an employee (of course, there is a downside if your company loses money).

- **You'll be working for (and with) yourself.** This might sound a lot like "you're the boss," but it's much more about whether or not you enjoy your own company. If being alone for reasonable amounts of time is a plus for you (as it is for many entrepreneurs), line this benefit up in the pros side of your spreadsheet.

THE DRAWBACKS

- **You're the boss.** Remember when I mentioned you'll be making all the decisions now? You'll also have to take complete responsibility for any missteps, failures, or flops. It's important to develop a thick skin.

- **You pay all the bills.** That includes your own health insurance, all office furniture, computer equipment, and anything else you'll need to maintain operations. New business owners can feel as overwhelmed as new home owners when the pipes freeze or fuses blow and there's no landlord to foot the bill anymore. To add to that stress, borrowing money might prove difficult for you if you don't have a proven track record. You'll have to establish a strong relationship with a financial institution.

- **Beware of laundry and fishing.** When you run your own show, you must devise ways to ignore mountains of laundry at home or turn down that last minute fishing invitation and instead concentrate on the hard work that will drive your burgeoning company toward success. The thing is, there may not be any pressing obligations that day, but the only way to procure more paying clients is to focus single-mindedly on expanding your business opportunities and ignore distractions.

- **Inherent risk.** This furthers my previous discussion on risk-taking. There is no way to avoid putting your personal livelihood on the line. Bad luck or bad timing could lead you to profound losses in income. The smart entrepreneur develops as many back-up plans as possible and learns to think on his or her feet.

- **It's lonely at the top.** Suddenly, for hours at a time, new business owners work alone at their computers with no morning hello, no office gossip or even a pat on the back for a job well done. If you are someone for whom social isolation might be a problem, it's wise to schedule weekly or even daily meetings with prospective clients to bridge the gap. Or you might consider renting an office with a like-minded group of professionals.

* * *

Ask E-Diva

Dear E-Diva,

We are small business owners who have billed a big business customer who is 10 days late past the 30 days net pay terms on the bill, and 40 days later they have not paid their corporate invoice. We have called them in the past; however, they always make us feel guilty. Is this normal? You see, they are a big corporation, and we were told they hate for us to call and we are a joke for calling their accounting department about our past due invoices.

What should we do?

Mr. Collection Caller

Dear Mr. Collection Caller,

To answer your first question, YES this is normal to call on your company's invoice(s). The answer to your last question: CALL!

To run your business, money is needed. For every dollar due you are paying for it, either through the bank from your credit line or through expected profits. Volume or margins are a must. Most of the time if you are dealing with people who never ran a business, it can be difficult to communicate business 101.

By the way, overhead must be paid (light bills, electricity, paychecks, etc.) for your company too. Cash flow is imperative in ALL businesses. Money moves in and out of businesses (flow).

If they (the corporate person you speak with) missed a paycheck because their corporation did not get the money in a timely manner, it would make an impact on them and the joke would be on them. Getting a weekly check from a corporation usually shields them from what makes a business run.

Don't let this discourage you from calling, and if your calls don't work, hire a collection expert or lawyer to handle this process for you. It may cost you, but going through the harassment is unnecessary.

Providing a service or product to any company should never be unappreciated. It should be team collaboration on both sides. Share with the staff person the terms of payment, the written agreement, or even the precedence of the past payment process or your industry standards. If that does not work, follow my aforementioned comments.

I have worked with large corporations that have filed bankruptcy or have had union problems, and it surprises me they don't remember that you worked with them when no one else would … but asking them for your money becomes a joke. Well, they might be having money problems and that's no joke; ask for your money! Smile at the dumb stuff… don't forget to thank them for sharing; this is a person who needs help! This is business!

There are uniformed people everywhere working in these companies, thank God it's not you. Running a business is no joke!

*The article below is from a collection site on the Internet (**www.seniormag.com**); maybe this can help you as well. It's from a magazine pertaining to a health care provider, but could be related to any industry.*

E-Diva

From Seniormag.com

We've all been there. Collections! You sent your bill, your customer owes you money, and they simply aren't paying it. They've turned you into a bill-collector. Maybe they've promised payment you, maybe they haven't. But the bottom line is that you are owed money and they are not paying.

Some people do their bill-collecting with a bit of yelling, toss in a few insults, and think they will somehow guilt or badger the client into coughing up the fees that are due. These credit collection tactics might occasionally work, but the relationship is gone and it can make it harder to collect. If there is any chance of ever doing business again, calling the debtor customer a "deadbeat", will pretty much burn that bridge.

Credit collections are probably one of the worst parts of owning a business. Nobody enjoys being a bill collector, dunning people up for payments, threatening their credit records, turning over their clients to a collection agency, or taking legal actions. For most of us, this is bothersome for several reason including the fact that we have almost certainly also lost a client in the process.

When you run your own business however, being a bill-collector is part of the process unless you are fortunate enough to have collected all your fees up front. Even then, there are those extraneous costs that are incurred that still must be invoiced and some people are simply going to want to rip you off.

Many small business owners are fearful that if they push collections too much, they will alienate their good client who will go elsewhere. They rationalize that if they keep providing services, the good customer will recognize the value of the services and do their part in keeping the business relationship.

CREDIT COLLECTIONS AND THE "GOOD CUSTOMER"

Let's destroy a "good customer" myth right here. If a customer isn't paying their bill, they are NOT a good customer, even if they are your only customer or if they owe you a lot. Customers that do not pay their bills are ones that you can do without, even if they are the nicest people in the world.

Bill collecting is particularly hard in the home care personal services industry, especially when dealing with frail seniors. There is something about collecting money from older feeble folks that is particularly distasteful, and their kids who should be responsible get particularly nasty when you've called dunning "Mom" up for the money.

So how can you avoid collections issues or speed up the process? Here are a few tips to get you going:

1) Sign a contract. No matter how or when you get paid, if you have a contract that spells out the provisions of the service and the fees that are payable, this eliminates a lot of questions and problems. Contracts are critical in setting payment terms.

   Many small business owners rely on verbal agreements. While this should work in an honorable world, often it doesn't. Small business owners are often fearful of being too demanding of their clients and are afraid to pull out the contract. For the most part, anyone who is fearful of signing a contract isn't going to be a good client anyway.

2) Shorten the billing cycle. Instead of 30 days, why not shorten it to 10 or 15, or even due upon receipt. This way, if you have a customer that isn't paying, you know it sooner than later, and you have a reason to call the customer about the payment sooner. If people have several smaller bills instead of one big one, they are also more likely to get them paid on time. They are also less likely to ruin their credit over a small one than a large one as well.

3) Look at your invoices again. Are the billing terms visible and clear? If the invoice due date is not obvious, you invoice will probably go into a stack to be paid "sometime". Being in the "sometime" stack is never a good thing. Also consider adding a late payment fee to the invoice. If money is tight, people prefer to make the payments on bills that will cost them the most if they are late. If there is no penalty and they don't think you will cut off service, your bill goes to the bottom of the stack.

4) Get paid upfront. Okay, that's pretty obvious, right? Some businesses can get away with it and some cannot. Much of it is also on how the concept of upfront payment is sold. Consider these two statements:

   A) *We usually ask for some amount of payment up front. Can you write me a check for $300?"*

   B) *"For new clients, we require the first week's payment in advance and then you will be billed weekly from that point on. The cost of service is $300 per week so I will need you to get me a check for that amount."*

   The first one sounds like it is optional or negotiable and almost being asked as a favor. The second one sounds like it is a matter of policy and then the speaker keeps going, assuming that the policy is acceptable. Note that the speaker does not "ask" for the check, he pulls the listener in as a partner to help finalize the agreement. "I need you to…"

5) At some point in the collections cycle, you will have done what you can do. It then becomes a "collection issue" and it is appropriate to turn the client over to a bill collector. You have reached the point where you can no longer salvage this business relationship. You can write or make all the phone calls you want, but the customer just isn't going to respond with a payment. Of course, if the customer has a problem paying their bill, why would you want to salvage the relationship anyway, right?

Collection agencies will take anywhere between 10-50% of the collected amount. That's huge! But it's better than going away without a dime and in smaller amounts; the cost can beat the hassles of going to court.

6) Small claims court is really your last resort and last chance at collecting the bill. If you don't push your claim to this point, you simply aren't going to collect from many deadbeats. Small claims processing fees can run from $30-70 and you can act as your own attorney. If you win, the judge will not only award you what you are due but award you the processing fees too.

The trick to winning in small claims court is to have all of your documentation with you. Without this, you will be hard pressed to win your case. Show up with contracts, any related memos and witnesses, invoices, payment reports, and correspondence from you or to you regarding payment.

It's not surprising that defendants will lie in court about what was said or agreed to. They will often try to modify the terms or reject any notion that they agreed to pay what you say they do. But if you have the documents to prove it, you will prevail.

* * *

There are some other ways of venturing into business. You may want to purchase a new business or invest in a franchise. Let's look at those options.

PURCHASING AN ESTABLISHED BUSINESS

This option provides you with a set location, product inventory, past profit analysis, experienced employees, and in all likelihood a marketing database of past customers. This is also one way to mitigate diving into the cold waters of new business ownership, for you very well may be able to work with the past owners during the transition period.

But similar to the disadvantages of buying a used car, you don't always know what you're getting.

You simply must scrutinize the financial reports of the company. The building could be outrageously outdated, and require more work (and money) than what it would cost to establish an entirely new location. And if the company is successful, why are they selling? Is the competition simply too fierce for you to gain a foothold? Ask yourself and the seller very difficult (and potentially uncomfortable) questions and seek the consultation of lawyers and other experienced professionals before signing anything.

PURCHASING A FRANCHISE

Perhaps the greatest advantage of buying a franchise is that your customers will already be familiar with a known brand. Purchasing a franchise also exhibits greater rates of success than buying a brand new business.

On the other hand, some franchisers (especially those pushing you to sign that contract) have less than pure motives. Again, ask the difficult questions, and never move forward without an attorney's review of the contract.

Finally, finding the right franchise for you could take a lot of work. You'll need to ask about all relevant fees and any existing training programs, not to mention royalties and purchasing restrictions.

This is where it's wise to think again about your personality. Do you want to start something brand new, a company of your own? Though it certainly has many advantages, franchising may not be for you.

Remember there are so many ways you can (and should) contribute your talents and experience. You might decide to stay put at your company and work on developing your professional skills — an immensely satisfying course of action. You could even decide to act as an "intrapreneur": Someone who dynamically strives to challenge established protocol, brainstorm new ideas for customers, and drive new revenue streams within their company.

Or maybe it's time to write that business plan and follow your long-cherished dreams of establishing your new business.

Whatever course of action you decide upon, remember to be true to yourself. This is the only avenue to true success.

17

Chapter Two

Tackling Your Business Plan Step by Step

" Sow a thought, reap an action; sow an action, reap a habit; sow a habit, reap a charac-ter; sow a character, reap a destiny."
– Chinese Proverb

From my years of being E-Diva and watching and listening to other entrepreneurs talk about their businesses, I've learned how important it is to have a plan. After all, you can have all the ingredients for success but that means nothing without a suitable recipe.

A plan is a suitable recipe.

That's particularly true of business plans. Time and time again, through my own experi-ences and those of others, I see how a solid business plan, the road map to your success, can turn your dreams into reality.

A good business plan forces you to analyze and critique your business.

And that's a good thing. It slows you down so you don't rush in and make bad decisions.

I remember I just could not stop fantasizing about my new business and I wanted to get started right away. Maybe that's the case with you (and if you've got an entrepreneur's blood running through your veins, I bet that is the case). If so, good! But you're not ready yet.

Before you make an appointment with your bank or invite a venture capitalist to a five-course lunch, read this chapter, and together, we'll walk through the elements of a great business plan.

Don't follow in the footsteps of so many new entrepreneurs who procrastinate (and even completely neglect) this vital exercise. Remember, 70% of small businesses close within two years. Without a fully fleshed out plan, businesses are much more likely to fail.

In this chapter I'll cover the overall format and content of your business plan (as well as the mistakes you must avoid). The big picture? When writing the core document of your new company, be as specific as possible but leave yourself plenty of room for growth. Let your enthusiasm serve you, but don't think for a minute that unsupportable claims won't be carefully investigated by investors. Keep it real. Remember this could very well be your draft entrée document into a number of different opportunities.

Besides being an absolute requirement for banks and investors, the exercise of writing your business plan will also better prepare you for the harsh realities (and thrilling opportunities) of running your own business.

In fact, researching and writing a business plan is the best way to immerse yourself in what you already know (like your product or service description and even competition analysis) and lots of things you might not (like the cost of appropriate facilities, infrastructure, cash flow, and accounting systems). In it, you'll be outlining concrete steps that can help you move forward based upon careful research and proactive long-term goals. Most importantly, you'll want to map out every conceivable way you can introduce your company's unbeatable solutions to live, paying customers.

SOLUTION . . . . MEET CUSTOMERS

Don't be dismayed when someone asks you about your value proposition. This favorite Master's of Business Administration term can be easily translated into two simple, but essential, questions:

- Why should customers buy your product?
- What distinguishes you from the competition (and no matter what you think, you have competition)?

You can't go wrong if you focus on your company's solutions and why customers will love what you offer. After all, customers are your reason for being, and must be defined, quantified (specifically in your market plan), and prioritized as you think through your business plan, for it is they who will determine your cash flow.

GETTING STARTED

Are you now convinced to sit down, brainstorm, and write your business plan before doing anything else? Well, I wouldn't blame you if you were still scratching your head and wondering, "Where do I start?" and "How in the world should I prioritize the necessary steps to write this business plan?"

The rest of this chapter will answer these and many other questions about the long road to self-employment. We'll cover many areas of business development, including choosing your business type, legal requirements, and marketing (among many other topics) in comprehensive detail. If you hire a consultant, don't rely on them to articulate your vision and write your business plan for you. Stay 100% involved in the process.

STEP BY STEP GUIDE TO SELF-EMPLOYMENT

- **Define your goals, both short-term and long-term.** Be clear about your purpose. Brainstorm. Here's your chance to put on your visionary hat. You will then be able to write a stellar introduction to your business plan, because you will clearly understand your company's overall purpose and be able to state it clearly. Make sure these goals can be measured. You should return to your goals regularly and evaluate your progress (or refine goals if they no longer apply).

- **Map out a clear route to each and every goal.** Here's your chance to put on your worker hat. Are you being realistic in setting your goals? How can you make your company's goals happen? What kind of obstructions are you likely to run into? How can you mitigate risk with back-up plans and forward-looking ideas?

- **Remember the 5 W's.** It helps to start with some basic who, what, when, where and which questions, such as:

  1. *Who* do you need? Do you want (or need) to hire a big staff (or any staff at all)? Who will you form a partnership with (if that is part of your plan)?

  2. *What* type of business will you start? What are your skills and experiences to back your business up (it is very important to take stock of these)? What are your resources? What are your tax advantages and disadvantages?

  3. *Which* insurance type best matches your needs? Which legal structure makes the most sense for your company?

  4. *Where* would the best location to set up shop be? Where will you obtain financing and necessary equipment?

  5. *Why* will your company succeed (back up your claims here with knowledge of and research about the market)?

- **Define your business type.** There are three most common types of business formations:

  1. *Sole proprietorship*: The "keep it simple" option, sole proprietorship does require a few initial moves, like finding a business location, registering, and hiring an attorney (choosing this option also means you'll pay the lowest legal fees).

  2. *Partnership*: Will you share equal responsibility (and investment) with another professional? The two choices within this option are general and limited partnerships, and though the former can be sealed with an oral agreement, I highly recommend obtaining a legal contract. You'll need to determine, among other things, how much equity will be invested by each partner, as well as compensatory plans.

  3. *Corporation*: (Limited Liability Corporation, C Corporation, S Corporation) Incorporating is the most complex and expensive option. Stock ownership enters into the picture, as those with the largest percentage of stock control the company. This also means that careful records must be kept of decisions made by a board of directors. Seek a professional for assistance upfront.

- **Find (or identify) your niche.** In other words, what makes your company so special? Who is your competition? What are your advantages? Can a demand for your product or service be created or capitalized upon?

- **Think marketing (and marketing means reaching people).** This goes back to the point I made in the last section: You could boast the best possible product in the world, but without securing any individuals to buy them, you won't get far. How will you reach and appeal to your market base? Research your company's demographic. One helpful way to think of your audience is to search in terms of market segments. Would they tend to be members of a specific professional organization? Is there a geographic region you could target? By thinking in terms of groups, you might be able to quantify your market base more easily, though of course you'll need to approximate.

- **SWOT it.** Here's a tried and true acronym, a powerful brainstorming tool to map out your company's Strengths, Weaknesses, Opportunities, and Threats (I recommend a competition analysis along with it). Deceptively simple, SWOT is a great way to start rounding out the big picture for your company. Make sure to stay positive. Balance threats with opportunities. Remember the old adage about God closing a door but opening a window? You can always turn a threat (like market saturation) into an opportunity (demonstrated demand for product or service). Where is the window opening for your new business?

- **Forecast the future.** Of course you don't have a crystal ball, but it's important to predict future market trends (based on research) and think about ways your product or service can find a safe place on that horizon.

MORE POINTED POINTERS

Now that you've brainstormed through the details such as the overall structure of your company, tax advantages, legal requirements, strengths, weaknesses, and marketing schemes, you're ready to move forward and write that business plan.

But just a few more pointers before we get down to the nuts and bolts.

One, your business plan is a living document. In your mind's eye you should put away the ink pen and take out the erasers. Know from the outset that your business plan can (and will) change as your company grows and you learn more about the market from experience. That said, every word of your business plan is important and must be substantiated. It should be a document broad enough to contain your enormous vision and specific enough to persuade investors.

Two, when you write, always focus on your company's strengths and what makes your company rare and necessary. The most successful companies identify their competitive advantage with supportable claims about why they are truly unique. What features or offerings makes your company strongest? As in other areas of life, in business it's easiest (and wisest) to move from strength to strength.

Three, think about your audience for the actual business plan before you write. Banks will want to see you've detailed ways to mitigate risk, whereas investors will want to discover countless reasons why your company will deliver them a great return on their investment. Some business plans are also written for internal audiences like a board of directors or advisors. So think about who you're writing for as you flesh out your business plan.

Finally, however you decide to write it, the following information must be in your business plan: Your company's history and background; a clear summary of your business concept

10 COMMON MISTAKES YOU CAN AVOID WHEN PLANNING YOUR NEW BUSINESS:

1. Not addressing a real market need. Offer solutions to real problems.

2. Overstating company's value without backup research. Stay on point; avoid exaggeration.

3. Trying to please everyone. Ever try to host a Thanksgiving dinner? Well, then you probably already know better than trying to make everyone happy. This is even more valid in the world of business. Focus on what you know you're good at, who you're writing for, and your strongest potential market(s), and the rest will follow.

4. Not including real marketing plans and analysis. You need to inform investors and bankers of how your product will enter the marketplace and gain traction

5. Claiming you have no competition. In that case, why should investors fund you? A perfectly reasonable line of logic could lead investors to the conclusion that if you have no competition, there is no demonstrated need (or market) for your product or service. The truth is you do have competition, though it might not be direct. Is there a company who offers something similar?

6. Redundancy and/or lack of detail.

7. Not including a risk analysis. Don't shy away from this hot potato. Instead, show your market confidence by facing every risk head on. Show investors you've thought this through and come equipped with real back up plans. Risks will emerge in almost every section of your business plan including market risks (will customers pay for your product?), technology risks (are you a company that has the resources to deliver on time?), operational risks (what could go wrong in day-to-day operations or customer service?), management risks (does your staff support your goals, will you be able to retain them, who will take over for you if necessary?), and legal risks (what's your liability?).

8. Procrastination. Timing is everything. Don't delay the process of writing your business plan. It often takes at least six months.

9. Forgetting about external review. Make sure an outsider gives this document a good once over. There's nothing like a new pair of eyes that are likely to see inconsistencies or even spot typos.

10. Forgetting about money ... and that means cash flow. It also means checks "in the mail" don't count. Where will you find cash to pay all your necessary expenses? You'd be surprised how many people forget about this.

and value proposition; marketing analysis and plans; financials; human resources plan; growth strategy; survival strategy; resource assessment (along with a possible return structure for investors); exit strategy; summary and appendices.

Now let's get started.

A STEP BY STEP GUIDE TO WRITING YOUR BUSINESS PLAN

Business plans should be anywhere from 15-30 pages long (but some business plans are as lengthy as 100 pages). Again, it depends upon your audience. But be kind to potential investors, who often see literally thousands of business plans a year. Make sure every word and section is necessary and strengthens the overall document. Also, if you're writing to obtain a $200,000 loan, the document must look different than one for a $15 million investment would.

Back up everything with research. You can obtain copious information from your local library, the Web, or a number of database services that offer relevant information on your market's growth, as well as industry snapshots. You can collect information from real live people and conduct interviews with experts in the field.

Once you have all this information compiled, you're ready to start writing.

- Begin with an introduction, and keep it direct and powerful. Describe your business and its goals with enough details to keep readers interested and convinced. Talk about the skills and advantages you bring to the market. You should also include information regarding the ownership structure of the business.

- In the marketing section, you should cover the product or service you offer and why it will be desirable to a tangible market. Define your target audience and who your typical customers would be. Provide market segment information and back your claims up with substantiated numbers. Show your ability to attract and retain a customer base. Do you have a branding plan? How will customers develop both familiarity and trust in your name?

- Probably the trickiest part of your business plan is financial strategy and management. You can't exaggerate, but you must demonstrate your ability to grow financially as a company. You'll need to make projections about your income statement and your cash flow and include a balance sheet. You'll need to assess the cost of products and delivery, as well as electricity and phone expenses. Among other subjects, you must discuss:

  1. A monthly operating budget

  2. Information on the sources of your capital and equity

  3. Your prospective return on investment for the first year

  4. Compensation schemes

  5. Balance sheet

  6. Risk mitigation

A consultant can really come in handy here, but don't be tempted to walk away and let the consultant tackle all the hard questions. You should provide all the real information such as rent, etc. Leave it to the consultant to organize the information you provide into colorful graphs and charts. Work closely with your consultant and you'll have a stronger document.

- Another nuts and bolts section is operations management. Here, you'll cover human resources issues and the way in which your business will be run on a daily basis. That means you'll review your hiring procedures. You'll also look at things like insurance and rental contracts, as well as equipment.

- In this day and age, it is essential to show you've thought carefully about a technology plan. It is striking to see how many new companies fail to recognize the importance of proactive thinking in this arena. What type of Web support will you need? Cover the technology risks here (like how much revenue might be lost if your network goes down for three days) and how you will install back up plans.

- In the plan's conclusion, restate your goals and the reasons it will succeed.

- An executive summary is a 1-2 page document summarizing the plan. Write this last, even though it usually will go first. Your executive summary should be punchy, relevant, and persuasive. By the way, writing an executive summary is absolutely essential, as many investors won't have time to read your entire business plan, but will look at a snapshot analysis to see if they should investigate any further.

* * *

Ask E-Diva

Dear E- Diva:

I went to some entrepreneurship training classes before my wife and I started our business. They spoke on subjects like looking for the proper location, marketing and sales of our product or service, financing, advertising, etc. However, one thing they never talked about was information technology in the workplace. E-Diva,, is technology important in the conversation of starting our business?

Mr. and Mrs. Not Informed

Dear Mr. and Mrs. Not Informed,

This is what amazes me about people taking classes for entrepreneurship: Why do you go to people who never ran a business?

I once assisted a social services organization to start an entrepreneur center, and after the center was up and running they cut me out of the program as a paid consultant. I just laughed and shook my head. What was so stupid about the whole thing was that they used my skills of 20-plus years and my good business name to get the money, but no one in the center had any for-profit business experience.

First, I would suggest you search for trainers and mentors with at least seven years of experience making money (with a real tax return to prove it). You are shaping your tools to go into the world to make a profit. Look up "profit" and look up "social service program" in your dictionary. Not for profit and for profit.

Whoa! See the difference?

So much for my pet peeve …

The worst thing anyone can do is start a business without a computer technology plan in their business plan. Yeah, I said it, a technology plan. Make sure your business growth and your technology growth are in sync. We are so used to having our lawyer, banker and accountant, but for some reason we forget our information technology person.

Having reliable technology in the workplace today is no longer a luxury, it's a necessity for running a successful business. Technology in the workplace is constantly improving, with new technology coming on the market all the time. Like a new car driving off the lot, it depreciates … quickly. Technology changes daily, so we must keep up for our business' sake.

This does not just mean computers, but software, postage machines, wireless environments, telephone systems and laser copying machines as well.

Mr. and Mrs. Not Informed, believe me, any technology from top to bottom is going to make your workload easier.

Remember, as Wilson Pickett once sang, "Don't let green grass fool you."

Sincerely,

E-Diva

* * *

Chapter Three

Financing Your New Business

" The important thing is not being afraid to take a chance. Remember, the greatest failure is to not try. Once you find something you love to do, be the best at doing it."
– Debbi Fields, founder of Mrs. Fields Cookies

Unless you're independently wealthy, you'll probably face the most common (though hardly unsolvable) problem when you start up your business: Securing reliable cash flow and obtaining financing sources.

Big questions and daunting procedures, such as "how do I apply for a loan?" or "what is a credit line?" or "what if I'm a victim of discrimination?" could discourage and frustrate the most enthusiastic of new business owners.

But they don't have to hold you back.

Again, if you do your homework and are prepared for the inevitable difficulties of this complicated process, you'll be well ahead of your colleagues. Let me tell you a bit about my own experience.

Twenty-five years ago, finding someone to mentor me – a single black mother in a small town – while I built what is now my multi-million dollar business didn't happen. In fact, finding a mentor for a minority woman with big business aspirations back then was harder than finding a needle in a haystack.

So when it came to obtaining finances, I struggled against the odds in my town, where there was a less than 1% success rate for minority businesses.

Needless to say, the setting was more than a little discouraging, especially when you consider my business goals were monumental (I was already thinking in terms of global business). I admit all of these obstacles scared me, but I wasn't going to let them stop me.

I started by going to a bank and asking for start-up money. Understand, I had no idea I would even need a credit line for this process. Meanwhile, my business was growing so fast I had to use credit cards to pay employees while I waited for customers to actually pay me, so cash flow became a major issue.

I persisted. I knew what I wanted and focused on just that: To succeed with my own business. It took a lot of trial and error to figure it all out, and while I made mistakes, I never stopped learning, and eventually reaped the rewards of this approach.

PLANNING FOR THE FUTURE

It's human nature … we'd much rather be doing than thinking.

But entrepreneurs may be the worst: We want that finished product in our hands (and don't forget the profits from the product).Thinking and planning is just so … well …boring.

But taking the time to plan for a proposed business might make the difference between a franchise that flops and one that sails out of the gate.

If business plans weren't so necessary for funding, we might never write them at all.

For an entrepreneur, a solid business plan is an extremely useful financial tool. Unfortunately, when most entrepreneurs walk into a bank with their hands out, most bankers brush just them off.

A business plan (presented clearly and confidently) can help turn the tide and get you the money you need to launch or grow your business. Show the bank in detail where your business is headed (both the long and short term) and lenders will feel more confident about giving you financing. Don't forget that showing your bank that you have sound accounting practices in your business plan will only help your chances.

Here are the top three reasons why you should write a business plan:

1. Preparing a business plan forces you to take an objective, critical, unemotional look at your business concept and whether all the aspects of your idea are working together.
2. The finished product, the plan itself, is an operating tool that (if properly used) will help you manage your business effectively on a daily basis.
3. The completed business plan communicates your ideas to others and provides the basis for your financing proposal.

You already know that going into business is risky — more than half of all new businesses fail within the first three years, and a I know a major reason is lack of planning.

I cannot overemphasize the importance of a good business plan. A plan helps pinpoint needs you might otherwise overlook (like a marketing budget that is unrealistic). It can help you spot unseen opportunities early (so you can take advantage of them right off the bat), or it can identify problems before they become a crisis. I know that once your business is underway there's no time to think about anything but the next 10 minutes, so an objective, comprehensive business plan can track your progress and identify where your company is weak and where it's working.

No matter how much of a creative genius you are, you've got to identify your company's business needs or you're not going anywhere. Sometimes the hardest part of writing a business plan is admitting that you need help writing a business plan. Don't worry, your self-esteem isn't going to suffer. You just can't do everything.

Finally, a business plan can forecast failure. Nobody likes to lose money, and if your proposed business is marginal at best, the business plan will reveal this truth.

Put simply, a business plan is the cheapest insurance policy against entrepreneurial impatience.

ANATOMY OF A BUSINESS PLAN

This is what I call the nuts and bolts. For some it's not very exciting, but like vegetables, it's good for you.

A business plan should describe in detail your company's goals, the strategies you'll use to meet them, potential problems and how you'll solve them, the organizational structure of your business and the amount of capital you'll need to finance it. A good business plan should cover the first three to five years of your company's existence, and it should be freely tweaked and modified as you progress (no business plan is etched in stone).

You can always rewrite a business plan if a good market opportunity arises.

Most business plans include seven basic elements:

1. An executive summary. Although this is the last part you should write, the executive summary is the first part the reader sees. Make sure it clearly states the nature of your business, and, if you're seeking capital, the kind of financing you need.

   The executive summary describes your business: Its legal structure (sole proprietorship, partnership, or corporation), the amount and purpose of the requested loan, repayment schedule, the borrower's equity share, and the debt-to-equity ratio after the loan, security or collateral is offered. You should limit the market value and estimated value or price quotes for any equipment you plan to purchase with the loan proceeds. The summary should be a half-page to a page in length (keep it short and businesslike).

2. A business description. This section gives the reader a more detailed description of your business concept (what and to whom you're selling). Specify your industry. Is it wholesale or retail, food service, manufacturing or service-oriented? Describe your product or service (make sure to emphasize any unique features that set it apart). Explain your target market, how the product or service will be distributed and your support systems (like advertising, promotions and customer service strategies). If you're seeking financing, explain why the money will make your business more profitable. Will you use it to expand, to create a new product or to buy new equipment?

3. Marketing strategies. Define your market's size, structure, growth prospect, trends and sales potential. Document how and from what sources you compiled your information. Then present the strategies you'll use to fulfill your sales objective.

   - *Price: Explain your pricing strategy and how it will affect the success of your product or service.*

- *Distribution: This includes the complete process of getting your product to the end user.*

- *Sales: Explain elements like sales presentations and lead generation.*

4. Competitive analysis. Detail your competitors' strengths and weaknesses, the strategies that give you the advantage and any particular weaknesses in your competition that you can exploit.

5. Design and development plans. If your product is already developed, you can skip this section. But if all you have so far is an idea (or if you plan to improve a product or service) this section is essential. The design portion describes your product's design and materials, and it provides diagrams. The development portion generally covers three areas — product, market, and organizational development. If you plan to offer a service, describe only these last two items and don't worry about the design or product.

6. Operations and management plans. Here you explain how your business will function on a daily basis. You describe the responsibilities of the management team, the tasks assigned to each department (if this is applicable) and the capital required. Go over key management personnel and their qualifications and explain what support personnel will be needed.

7. Financial factors. You knew it was coming — this is the math part, where you present your financial statements, including the following:

- *An income statement detailing your business' cash generation capabilities. It projects things like revenue, expenses, capital (in the form of depreciation) and cost of goods. Develop a monthly income statement for the business' first year, quarterly statements for the second year and annual statements for each year thereafter for the term as indicated in your business plan.*

- *A cash flow statement that details the amount of money going into and coming out of your business (monthly for the first year and quarterly for each year thereafter as specified in the plan). The result is a profit or loss at the end of each period. Both profits and losses carry over to the next column to show a cumulative amount. If your cash flow statement shows you consistently operating at a loss, you probably need additional cash to meet expenses.*

- *A balance sheet showing the business' assets, liabilities and equity over the period specified.*

BROTHER, CAN YOU SPARE $100,000?

With your well-written, detailed business plan in hand, you're ready to scour the city in search of financing. If you're one of the lucky few who doesn't need outside money, then you can proceed immediately to the next stage: Writing a marketing plan.

For a one-person shop, you might simply raid your bank account or credit card for $2,500 in start-up money (enough for a new computer, some letterhead and a coffee maker).

However, I know that no matter what your current financial situation, there usually comes a time when a business is ready to expand beyond an entrepreneur's ability to fund it. This is when you must go calling: To the bank, to family, to venture capitalists and to anybody else with a spare $500,000 burning a hole in their savings account.

There are no hard-and-fast rules. A friend of mine in San Francisco started up a home safety equipment firm. With his developed idea for an emergency safety ladder, he decided to bypass the venture capital route to get his company off the ground.

So he sold 30% of the company to individual investors — a group of professors he knew from his days at business school.

When I asked him how he started his business so quickly he told me, "Having a network is the most important thing in getting a business off the ground, financially." Since he went to business school and joined an alumni group he had already established a network.

But before entering into a financial agreement, my friend decided to first demonstrate his emergency safety ladder to retail giants like Kmart and Sears. When they responded favorably, he knew he had a viable product (and that he'd need money fast to fill the large orders they requested).

You always want to let investors know where their money is going. I know you can easily get flooded with questions (What do the investors get? What are our objectives? What are the marketing plans?), so when the relationship grows more complicated you need to keep a clear plan in your head.

I remember my friend telling me his initially supportive professors were getting cold feet. Their questions stretched on for months and there came a point where he told them time was running out and there would be no more questions — only money. He told me sometimes you really have to jolt the investors into making that decision. Investors need to be reassured and that takes time.

When dealing with investors my friend imparted this piece of wisdom: "Don't give investors three months to read a business plan."

He advised me to give them 24 hours, and not to give them too much time to reconsider.

One of his investors had signed an agreement that made him an investor, and when asked six months later what he had signed he didn't even know. The investor just trusted him and knew the product was good. He was making decisive decisions based on the individuals involved.

With a lot of money also comes the urge to spend it. Ask yourself: Do I need to have the best computers or the best office furniture? My friend reminded me to think cheap and sooner or later, you take pride in budgeting and saving money.

Four years and two rounds of financing later ($250,000 and $350,000, respectively), my friend was in business to the tune of $1 million in sales revenues.

30

* * *

Ask E-Diva

Dear E- Diva:

I am thinking about leasing computer equipment for my business. What do you think? Have you ever done this before? I need your advice.

Ms. Leasing

Dear Ms. Leasing,

To answer your question, I think leasing could be a great idea. However finding a reputable leasing company is really important.

A good leasing companies offer the following:

- *No sizable down payments; usually your first and last payment are required in advance.*
- *No additional collateral required.*
- *Preservation of cash flow.*
- *The lowest payment method when you are in need of new equipment.*
- *Multiple pieces of equipment from multiple vendors with only one payment.*
- *Structured payments, (seasonal, quarterly, etc.).*
- *Tax advantages.*

The bottom line is, leasing allows you to use your money without touching your bank account. You will have a monthly payment and a usage of the equipment.

So I have given you the educational side of the leasing process; of course I have had my own bad experiences…

I was recommended by a bank to a leasing company who basically had a friendly and probably a cash-back relationship with the local banks. I say that because everything was wrong about this leasing company.

To begin with, they made me guarantee my home and checking account. Before the equipment was out of the box, they made me sign a statement saying it was in perfect condition and working well (of course, the equipment did not work).

31

The bank did not try to work with me to resolve my issues with the leasing company, and the leasing company convinced the bank that I was crazy. I refused to pay the leasing company, assuming they would come get the equipment and replace it. Instead, they repossessed the equipment and reported me to the credit bureau, which lead to a bad mark my company's credit report.

Finally, the guy who owned the leasing company turned out to be the town alcoholic with shady practices in business, of course with friends in the banking business. But the pompous male bankers loved him; bad reputation and all, and this little girl was going to be wrong no matter what.

To sum it up, make sure the referral source is legitimate and not getting paid off by the bank or banker. Investigate, investigate and investigate!

Leasing can be a good thing. Since the bad experience, I have had a good experience.

E-Diva

* * *

KEY TIPS

A good rule of thumb is to discount nothing (and no one) in the preliminary brainstorming stages. Financing can come from a vast number of people and institutions, including your family and friends.

However, in all cases, you should strive to make the process wholly professional and for obvious reasons always respect the money (and time) of others.

It's best to pursue parallel funding from several sources, including your own savings, family and friends, potential investors and bank loans. So it makes sense to hire an attorney to help you with payback terms, or you can draft your own terms of agreement to repay any loans.

One thing I do know: Disputes over money can make or break a relationship, so be mindful! You'll also want to look as professional (re: prepared!) as possible, and an attorney can help you in this realm.

Here are some more specific suggestions about where to start looking for money:

- Personal savings. Use your own savings to finance many up front costs. Saving up over the years can give you a head start and if available, is obviously the best option when looking for funding sources.
- Family members and friends. Here's a group of your most staunch supporters and loyal allies. These familiar individuals are far more likely to loan you money without

interest or at a far lower rate than a bank (you'd be surprised how many companies started with help from personal friends or family). However, these are also the same people who might take you a little less seriously; maybe they even knew you when you were in diapers. That's all the more reason to present them with a repayment plan that's satisfactory, along with a neatly organized business plan. You don't want to lose their friendship and loyalty. It's best to approach your family and friends with a list of funding options. Don't play with anyone's money, including loans from your mother or father.

- Angel investors or venture capital firms. Be forewarned: These investors are usually more inclined toward large experienced businesses, but that doesn't mean they won't sometimes take a calculated risk on a really good idea and an impressive new business owner.

- Finance companies. According to the Small Business Administration, finance companies are consistent backers of new small-sized companies. Benefits of using a finance company include their flexibility and longer lease times. They can also provide you with funding more quickly. On the other hand, finance companies charge much higher interest rates.

- Banks and credit unions. This route requires you to write an effective loan proposal. It's helpful to remember exactly what banks are looking for so you know what to emphasize in your application for loans.

WHAT BANKS ARE LOOKING FOR

The information that follows will give you a heads-up on what more traditional financial institutions will ask for when you apply for lines of credit or loans through the Small Business Administration (SBA).

Since you need to know what you have to know before applying for a business loan through the SBA, here are just a few important points to follow up on. This will start you off, so, of course, contact the SBA and go through their complete check list (located on-line at www.sba.org).

For both types of loans (short-term and long-term), your business (or business-to-be) requires the following documentation before your loan request can be evaluated:

- A business profile. This is a written statement; a document describing the type of business you own, and includes details such as annual sales, number of employees, length of time in business and specifics of ownership.

- Loan request. This is a description of how the loan funds will be used. This statement should include purpose, amount and type of loan.

- Collateral. This gives the lender a description of the collateral you're offering to secure the loan, including equity in the business, borrowed funds and available cash.

- Business financial statements. These are complete financial statements for the past three years, as well as current interim financial statements.

- Personal financial statements. These are statements of all the owners, partners, officers and stockholders who own 20% or more of the business.

Be sure your financial statements are carefully prepared and up-to-date. The strength and accuracy of your financial statements will be the primary basis for the lending decision to go in your favor.

The most important documents in your financial statements are:

- Balance sheets from the last three fiscal year-ends.
- Income statements revealing your business profits or losses for the last three years.
- Cash flow projections indicating how much cash you expect to generate to repay the loan.
- Accounts receivable and "payable aging," breaking your receivables and payables in to 30-, 60-, 90- and past 90-day old categories.
- Your personal financial statements, along with statements from your business partners listing all personal assets, liabilities and monthly payments, and your personal tax returns for the past three years.

* * *

Ask E-Diva

Dear E-Diva,

I went to the bank for a business loan and they asked me for a personal financial statement. What is a personal financial statement? Is there something I could use to check financial worth? Can you help me?

Ms. Not Financially Savvy

Dear Not Savvy,

When you go to any financial institution, they normally look at your net worth, and

if you have an existing business that business' net worth. How do you get to the net worth? Take all your assets and subtract the figure from your liabilities.

Really, we all need to master our money, whether in business or not. Recently

I read a book called, "Master Your Money Type" by Jordan E. Goodman.

What I enjoyed about the book was that it was written for people like me who love to read but hate the authors who write so you can't understand it. He breaks it down. In the book you will find all the tools you need to generate a personal financial statement, cash flow statement and debt to income worksheet, asset worksheet, liability worksheet, and even a yearly budget worksheet.

Also in this book, there are tons of resources, publications, organizations, and Web sites.

So enjoy!

But back to your concern, the bottom line is to do your homework before you go to the bank. Be prepared if asked for collateral (security pledged for the repayment of the loan). Security interest is any interest in a property that secures the payment of an obligation.

Other advice:
- *Investigate the bank and the banker, just like they would investigate you.*
- *Investigate the interest rates.*
- *Investigate the bank's assets and liabilities*

35

- *Investigate the banker; make sure he or she has been fair when it comes to interest group.*

5. Make sure you understand any document you may sign; if need be, get your attorney involved.

DON'T SIGN UNTIL YOU UNDERSTAND WHAT YOU ARE SIGNING!

Lots of Luck. Working with a banker and banks with integrity can be rewarding.

E-Diva

* * *

WHAT TO INCLUDE A LOAN PROPOSAL (IN A NUTSHELL)

- Business name and address
- Names of principals and their social security numbers
- Purpose of the loan (be as specific as possible about what it will be used for)

- Amount of money you need (be exact)
- Business description: This should include what kind of business you're looking at starting or expanding, history, number of employees and current business assets, ownership and legal structure.
- A summary of management: Offer a short description on each principal, including background and education, experience, skills and accomplishments.
- A summary of the market: Demonstrate knowledge of your product and where it fits in the market, competition and role in the overall marketplace. Sketch a customer profile and how your business can fulfill customer needs.

HOW BANKS WILL REVIEW YOUR LOAN PROPOSAL (IN A NUTSHELL)

First and foremost, they want to see proof they will be repaid. This means they will investigate your credit.

Having at least 25 to 50% of your funding from outside sources will strengthen your case. Banks also want to see that you have sufficient experience to pursue business enterprise and suitable cash flow for the business to run.

PITCHING TO AN INVESTOR

It's more than a little unnerving to walk into a meeting with the sole purpose of convincing a potential investor to spend a whole lot of money on your new business. However, if you focus on a few suggestions gained from experience and research, you'll be well prepared and far less nervous.

Be realistic. If you have a great idea but little entrepreneurial experience, you still might be able to convince an "angel investor" to back you. However, you must present realistic sums. Think in terms of $20,000 rather than $100,000.

It's nothing personal. Remember, you are selling potential investors your business idea and should craft a strong pitch about why you believe so strongly it. If they say no, it's nothing personal. In fact, you should listen carefully to just why a potential investor rejects your plan and keep it in my mind when planning for your next pitch. But don't take every rejection to heart. Investors see countless pitches, and after all, they might have had a headache that day. Persistence is the key to success in business.

Craft a strong pitch. Your pitch, or elevator speech, should boil down exactly what makes your idea the next big thing. Clearly outline the market and explain the cultural shift that is paving the way (and creating outrageous demand) for your product or service. Include statistics that show you've done your homework, but don't get lost in dull, dry facts. Your pitch needs to have considerable punch backed by numbers – because most importantly, you need to sell investors on why this is the smartest investment they can make right now.

Timing. Timing is everything. You'll need to demonstrate your business plan realistically assesses market demand and correlates bringing your product to market. It will do investors no good that you rightly anticipate the next technology jump if your timing is off by 10 years.

Ask yourself (and answer) all the hard questions first. That way you'll be prepared when investors inevitably challenge any weaknesses in your plan. Even better, you can identify any weaknesses and improve upon them before the meeting. However, investors are likely to play devil's advocate (after all you're talking about spending a lot of their money) so prepare solid answers before you're in the hot seat.

Accept the odds. Be optimistic, but be realistic. It is very difficult to obtain funding from investors. Contrary to popular belief, most new companies don't initially get funding from investors.

Have fun with it. This might seem like odd advice, but the truth is we are often at our best when we relax and enjoy what we're doing … even when that means being grilled by a room full of business people. Trust your instincts and stay committed to learning from the experience and you can't go wrong. Demonstrate your enthusiasm for what was only a dream not too long ago. After all, you've come a long way!

Here are some of the top traits investors are looking for:

- Experience. Show all relevant experience to investors.
- Market knowledge about real live customers. Do your homework.
- Enthusiasm and commitment. It takes tenacity and passion to launch a new business. Show investors that you're 100% committed.

- Flexibility. Don't be too rigid. Markets (like people) change. Show investors you can roll with the punches.
- A strong business model.

DEALING WITH "NO"

In some cases, there are responses that might sway naysayers. For instance, if a prospect says they don't have enough money to give you, ask for a smaller amount. Or say they're not totally convinced your business will take off, despite a thorough business plan. Offer them collateral so a potential investor will see their bases will be covered.

Finally, if you are talking to a friend, maybe they've been burned by a past acquaintance to whom they lent money. Show them in writing what will happen if you miss or are late with payments. Ease their concerns.

It's important to remember there are times when you actually should say no to loans. First of all, always trust your instincts: There's probably a good reason if something seems to be too good to be true. If you suspect a relationship might be negatively impacted by a loan, you should walk away from the money.

Many new entrepreneurs also make the mistake of selling too much of their company too soon. You don't want your initial vision to be lost before it even has the chance to be fully realized. It's important that you don't take money from investors you don't know anything about.

And avoid asking for more money than you need. Be realistic about what you need right now, not for the next 10 years.

One loan type you should be particularly wary of is a bridge loan. You'll know it's a bridge loan if it has an inordinately high interest rate and an enormous debt for the entrepreneur if the company fails.

Avoid it, no matter what.

* * *

Ask E-Diva

Dear E-Diva,

I have a dream to start my own business. Like a lot of women, I don't have the money to get through start-up costs, etc. Is there some organization that helps single women get loans? What do I have to do? What kind of background info do they need?

A Could-Be Martha Stewart

Dear Could-Be Martha,

When I teach my classes on being an entrepreneur, money is always a hot issue.

There are so many ways to get money, if you have an idea for a viable business or already have started a business that's a profit-maker.

Where to go? I can honestly say that if you keep running into brick walls with local bankers, try outside of your community to get funding.

I would encourage you to look at the Small Business Administration's official Web site (www.sba.gov), or to call their answer desk at (800) 8-ASK-SBA.

When it comes to financing, take it step by step, learn from every piece of feedback you receive, and stay the course. With the right approach, persistent efforts, and a solid business plan, you're destined for success.

E-Diva

* * *

Chapter Four
Putting Together Winning Teams

" We were young, but we had good advice and good ideas and lots of enthusiasm."
– Bill Gates, founder of Microsoft Corporation

If you're anything like me, you'll find that starting and running your own business will be extremely rewarding, but also extremely time consuming and physically taxing.

This is not to say it will not be an incredibly rewarding professional and personal growth experience. It simply means that you are going to need some help along the journey.

When I started my business, I knew I needed a core business team. Because let's face it, every small business eventually needs to fill fundamental roles. The key is to pick your resources with care and bring them into the decision-making process as soon as you're committed to going forward. You really have to listen to their advice and build a solid underlying business framework.

It's a dynamic process. As your business grows and thrives, you will have the need for additional teams; small groups of internal employees empowered to tackle important projects. You want to know how to form great teams and keep them motivated and productive.

In order to staff your teams with quality workers, you need to have a suitable hiring system. Such a system will insulate your firm from the effects of employee turnover and prepare you for periods of expansion.

Maybe you'll find an employee has become more of a liability than an asset (goodness knows that's happened to me once or twice). In that case, you'll also need to know the proper procedures to terminate employment. Firing someone correctly minimizes the chances of legal repercussions and reduces the effects on the morale of your remaining staff.

We will cover all these areas integral to your organization's prosperity in this chapter. Get set as we begin with your core business team.

THE CORE BUSINESS TEAM

These are the people you will most likely start discussions with once you have a good idea of the type of business you want to run. Think of them as a sounding board for your approach to operations. Utilize them to avoid pitfalls and to find the best shortcuts to success.

First and foremost on the team is the accountant. Your business will need one, at least part-time.

A good accountant does more than record sales figures and check inventory. When looking for an accountant, make sure they have a CPA (Certified Public Accountant) designation for the state in which you are operating. The CPA title indicates the accountant has not only been formerly educated and at least holds minimal work experience in their discipline, but has gone on to pass a specific test requiring a deep understanding of the profession (any accountant who has these qualifications will display the CPA designation after his or her name).

The justifications for a good accountant are many. You will have to pay taxes. How much and when can significantly affect the cash flow of your business. Do you know all the items that are deductible and under what conditions? Your accountant will (or should).

Speaking of cash flow, a good accountant can help you plan your billing and collection cycle so money is available to pay your bills as they come due. Many start-up businesses fail not because they don't have enough customers or market a poor product or service, but rather because they don't have the cash to pay their debts on time. A good accountant will plan ahead so this doesn't happen.

Accountants can help you find hidden cash through proper budgeting. They are tremendously useful during strategic planning to determine if and when you should increase the headcount of your workforce or make the purchase of costly new assets. Use your accountant to realize your profitability potential.

A lawyer or legal representative is another key team member. Business in today's society is litigious. That is simply a characteristic that exists, and one of which you must be aware. Even small businesses are required by law in many cases to have certain documentation filed, to follow specific hiring practices, to disclose certain types of information and to comply with environmental, trade and commerce laws.

Do you know all the applicable laws your organization must be aware of as dictated by the state or states in which you operate? Do you know the existing or potential laws governing your industry? Will you need to draft such things as legally binding contracts?

It is unwise to imagine that your business will never have a legal problem with a customer or an employee. A lawyer can help you create a risk management plan to deal with the most likely legal situations that could affect your company. This way, you can prevent problems or prepare for the correct actions to reduce potential losses before it is actually necessary.

Legal representation may be part of your organization through maintaining in-house counsel (usually reserved for larger companies or corporations) or as is more likely in a small business, maintaining a legal contact to work on an as-needed basis or through a retainer or other formal arrangement.

41

The knowledgeable insurance agent is another valuable core team member. If your business has costly assets or operates in a risky industry, you will want proper coverage. In addition, the geographic placement of your assets may warrant special coverage options if natural disasters are likely. A good agent is someone who can assist you in picking the right policies for your business type. They should be involved in reviewing existing coverage as the business grows or on a periodic basis to determine if new economic conditions warrant changes.

In the event a worst-case scenario plays out, you want to be able to replace equipment and resume operations as quickly and easily as possible. A good insurance agent will put you in a position to be able to do that.

Along with the previously mentioned specialties, you may want to have a listing of virtual resources. I call them virtual because they represent information that may not be located in any one individual but distributed through various organizations or resources.

For example, you may be an exceptional financial planner, but if you don't know much about marketing, your name might never become known. How can you fill in this deficiency? Use quality free or low-cost services through agencies such as the Small Business Administration (SBA) or organizations like the Service Corps of Retired Executives (SCORE). Consult with professors of business or their graduate students at local universities (and browse the business libraries).

Utilize information available on the Internet. Using theses options should provide you with essential basics and present some best practices for a variety of business disciplines. You may also end up making contacts with people (consultants who can help you with specific problems — we'll discuss consultants further later).

Here are some useful Web links:

- Small Business Administration (SBA)
  www.sba.gov
- Service Corps of Retired Executives (SCORE)
  www.score.org
- Internal Revenue Service (Small Business Resources)
  www.irs.gov/businesses/small/index.html
- Small Busineees.com
  www.smallbusiness.com/wiki/Main_Page

Assembling and Motivating Winning Teams

Once it is up and running and has passed the initial growth phase, every business depends on internal teams to get work done. It is therefore highly critical that you know how to make your teams more successful. The time used for proper team formation and maintenance will easily pay for itself through the benefits gained.

The number one rule — if you want the greatest chance of success — is form great teams.

Accomplish this feat by determining a team's membership based on the best people for the task at hand — not solely by who is available. If your best people aren't working on the most significant projects, what do you have them working on? Picking the best emphasizes the point that management is making a commitment to excellence. Consciously or unconsciously, people will also assess the quality of their teammates in determining the importance of a project or assignment.

Next, give your teams clearly communicated goals. Management must align the team's goals with the company's mission, vision and values (some good information on this subject is at **humanresources.about.com/cs/strategicplanning1/a/strategicplan.htm**).

Eliminate potential contradictions. Otherwise, a high performance team may find itself spending time engaged in unproductive conflict with the organization as a whole. Once suitable goals are established, the context of the work – its ultimate benefit to the company, the projected timeframe and the specific details of the final deliverables –

needs to be clearly articulated.

Make communication of the goals a two-way process — meaning not only is information flowing from top management down, but questions posed by the team to management are heard and answered upfront in a timely manner. Have your teams take ownership of final goals once they are formally agreed upon with management. Ownership means the team itself accepts the responsibility for the ultimate success or failure of the assignment.

The real power of a team will come from the collaborative efforts of its members; the synthesizing of different ideas and perspectives, not simply putting a group together in hopes that at some point each person in turn will blurt out correct answers. Newly-formed teams need time to meet and establish ground rules for how they will perform their work.

Let the team make its own decisions. Roles for each person need to be addressed. Will there be a single leader or several leaders for the team? Is everyone's input equal in weight or does someone have final say? Will some members only be utilized part-time or only during certain stages of the work?

Have the team discuss methods of conflict resolution and professional courtesy in their dealings with each other. Many teams create an official charter that defines the group's mission, vision and values (in alignment with the organization's), along with the details about how they are going to work together (if the project is complex, spread out over a long period of time or contains many unknown elements, the charter should include a section on removal and acquisition of new members as needed).

You can learn more about setting up successful teams online at: **humanresources.about.com/od/involvementteams/a/?once=true&**.

MANAGEMENT'S CONTINUING RESPONSIBILITIES TO TEAMS

Management should not simply let teams run off to finish a job. Teams require cooperation between management and the workers.

Upper management should clarify how the team's work should be prioritized in relation to each individual's other organizational roles. Is the team a full-time assignment for its members, or is time split between group work and individual duties? If member time is split, then it is management's responsibility to prioritize work to minimize conflicts.

For example, if a critical project test run of a new service will occur at the end of the month, but this is at odds with the need for some of the members to close the books — how do individuals know which task is more crucial?

Management must plainly articulate which is more important, the monthly accounting work or project milestones. If management has taken the time to assess and correctly align the goals of its core businesses and its projects, management should have a prioritized portfolio of tasks (both project-oriented and those essential to on-going business) to assist in organizing their subordinates' work. When people know what is expected and the order it is required, they can better plan their time and efforts.

Regular meetings can be a great way to facilitate good relations.

* * *

Ask E-Diva

Dear E-Diva,

My job mandates that I set up meetings and run them for my corporation. I have never had this type of responsibility. How do you run an effective business meeting? Can you give me some pointers?

Meeting Novice

Dear Meeting Novice,

Actually, many studies have shown more time we wasted in meetings than in any other business activity. I've been told it's been estimated that most upper management (30-40%) spend much time in meetings. The kicker is, these meetings are only 40-50% effective.

So improving the efficiency of the meeting is the objective; this increases the bottom line for your business.

The first step is to recognize why you having the meeting. Who are the players? And what is the ultimate goal? Before calling a meeting, decide whether it is really necessary. Other options available might be sending an e-mail or memo. It's the responsibility of the solicitor (that's you) to determine the need for calling the meeting and who should attend.

Secondly, invite as few participants as possible to the meeting. You must check the calendars of the participants, reserve the meeting room and assign a meeting facilitator to be in charge of the agenda.

Thirdly, leading a meeting requires establishment of rules. Most meetings are governed by Robert's Rules of Order to minimize confusion and to promote a code of conduct.

Here are some tips for running good meetings:

- *Start on time.*
- *Review the agenda.*
- *Focus on listening and seek understanding before disagreeing.*
- *If you agree to do a task, be accountable to the group.*
- *Agree as a group not to engage in distracting conversations and non-productive behavior.*
- *Allow participants to disagree; however, after the group has made a decision it needs to be supported by everyone in the group. Negative gossip, passive resistance and sabotaging are not acceptable.*
- *Celebrate and reward success. And don't forget to thank your members for attending and for all their efforts at the meeting.*

Meetings are the key to having a successful business. Good luck! And knock 'em dead…

E-Diva

* * *

Now let's address motivating desired team behavior.

A very important and applicable rule to remember is simply that people do what they are rewarded for. If team success (the attainment of the team's goals) is compensated in the form of a financial bonus, vacation time, praise and promotion or access to future project opportunities of their choice, members will be enticed to perform together as a team.

If, however, management continues to compensate individuals for working as individuals, they are undercutting the potential power of the team. It is management's responsibility to structure or change the compensation system to promote teamwork and the subsequent collaborative behaviors they want workers to exhibit.

Sustaining winning teams requires management to adopt a position of support. Increase team productivity by providing the necessary tools to complete the job and removing organizational obstacles to their progress. Management should actively work to provide the necessary budgetary considerations, information technology and access to data or training that will be required. It should also work in conjunction with the team to open doors and form connections to key people or contacts that can propel the project along.

As teams progress in their assignments, management needs to provide the team with constructive feedback. The team should be notified if their performance is not meeting expressed expectations (give specific details) and they should be praised for achieving milestones and the ultimate final project goals. Feedback should be given on a continual basis throughout the team's assignment (choose a sensible time interval to meet consistently, based on the total assignment length).

Again, the communication should be two-way with opportunities for the team to express concerns, request removal of obstacles or acquire additional resources.

As projects wind down, management should eliminate future job uncertainty in team members.

When dealing with temporary teams (those created to address a limited business need that will eventually disband), let members know what their responsibilities will be after the work is done.

People develop routines where they begin to feel comfortable. This is not a bad situation, but when the future is uncertain, teams may stretch out the completion of their project to extend their comfortable routines just a little longer. As management, you want to deploy good people onto other important work. Give team members advance notice of their next project, new team assignments or confirm their return to regular business tasks prior to a project's end.

IMPROVING TEAMS

Finally, once the current project is completed, successful teams improve by conducting post-mortems and evaluating members' performances.

The post-mortem (conducted after a project is either completed or terminated) requires the team to brainstorm and list those team actions, team processes and external factors they felt were effective, and also those they found to be ineffective or that made the initiative less than optimal.

Simply use a whiteboard or other writing surface and create two columns (one for the positives and one for the negatives). Record everyone's input about the project. Repeat the same exercise a second time with a representative (or representatives) from management present. This will provide lists from both the team's and management's perspective.

Compare and compile both lists, record the information and put the best practices into play on the next team project.

Self-evaluation is important. The team should conduct its own member evaluation internally.

Put each member in the spotlight while the other members tell them what they did well and what they should continue to do or do more of. The spotlighted person is then told by team members those areas where they could improve (wording it in this way enables you to frame negative comments such as "she talks too much out of turn" as "she would benefit from listening more when others are speaking").

The team evaluations need not be recorded formally, and comments should remain within the team itself. Individuals looking to improve their performance should record the comments pertinent to them and review consistently after each project to identify progress.

Some helpful information on giving positive feedback can be found online at:

- **http://humanresources.about.com/cs/communication/ht/Feedbackimpact.htm**
- **http://humanresources.about.com/cs/communication/ht/receivefeedback.htm**

Successful Hiring

Any business worth its salt needs good people to staff its internal teams. As your business grows, the need for talent will become almost constant.

So how do you obtain the best resources?

Here's my take on it. Make all your hiring decisions based on a well-defined business need. This means have a specific role you expect a new hire to fulfill that directly or indirectly contributes to the company's bottom line.

A direct contributor unequivocally increases profits or reduces expenses. An indirect contributor actively supports individuals or roles that are making a direct contribution (they make someone else's role more effective or efficient). Make sure a new worker's role is in line with the organization's goals as a whole.

Once you have a business need, start describing the position through listing the essential knowledge, skills and abilities (KSA's) required to perform the role.

Knowledge is specific information pertaining to an area. Skills are psychomotor tasks or functions that an employee can perform (typing, dictation, listening, calculating, etc.)

Abilities are behaviors that are used to produce a tangible service or product.

Leadership and management are abilities, and they incorporate the other two characteristics, knowledge and skills, to produce a useful and desired end result.

It may be easy to get carried away listing every KSA under the sun for a position, but your chances of finding candidates with all these attributes is slim (or may require considerably more time than the position is ultimately worth). Stay focused only on the essential ones; those that are absolutely necessary to properly perform the work. You can list those are nice to have, and if you find them in a candidate already possessing the essentials consider it a bonus, but don't let their absence delay the hiring process.

47

Also, remember that educated people or motivated individuals can develop KSA's. If the position you need to fill is crucial and candidates with the minimum qualifications can't be found but someone intelligent could be brought up to speed quickly, consider them. Someone who can be brought up to speed exhibits the willingness to learn, high intelligence and has high energy levels.

When viewing candidates, remember skills and abilities are transferable across industries and job classifications. Motivated individuals can learn a new profession's terminology and idiosyncrasies. Someone adept at legal research can make a transition to marketing research. A technical professional with exceptional analytical and mathematical skills can work with numbers in a banking or a financial setting. A project manager for a grocery chain can apply their logistical and organization skills to a department store.

Don't narrow your search criteria so much that you unnecessarily spend additional time and effort looking for perfection.

A common hiring practice is to try to obtain the very best existing "superstars" to fill positions. Truthfully, this is not always the best practice and in many instances it is completely unnecessary.

Superstars are encountered less frequently than the average worker, hence the superstar designation. They generally require greater time to locate and recruit. Superstars have greater mobility in the workforce; they are highly coveted. This in-demand status means they may have considerable opportunities to jump ship for a continuous stream of better positions.

48

Superstars tend to have their own way of doing things, which frequently means they are not team players — they don't have to be. Superstars usually garner higher salaries and compensation, which can lead to resentment among colleagues, as well as take away from your bottom line.

Lastly, the designation of superstar is subjective. If someone was wildly successful in a certain position with another employer, there is no guarantee their performance will be duplicated in the new scenario, particularly if your company uses a different approach.

So what is a viable alternative to hiring a superstar? Obviously, no one wants to be known as an organization composed of average workers. First, make sure you've thoroughly analyzed the roles for which you are hiring. Have you made sure that they fit a business need and fit with the organization's objectives as a whole? When you answer yes to these questions, look at the KSA's (described previously) for the position. When you look for candidates, look for those people that already have the KSA's required or can easily and quickly acquire them. They are good candidates.

Why do you approach recruiting in this manner? Simple: Because it provides several logical business benefits. Assessing good candidates will generally reduce the time to find people because you are not obsessed with finding a superstar.

Typically the cost (in terms of salary and bonuses) is less than hiring a superstar. By recruiting someone with the minimum KSA's (or the ability to acquire them) you have the opportunity to grow the individual's career. Remember, having the minimum qualifications doesn't mean they are not acceptable workers.

If you have accurately defined the needed KSA's for the position, the candidate possessing them should be able to perform the role. Just because they didn't start out as a superstar doesn't mean they can't finish as one. By providing in-house training, you have greater control of their working skill set and at the same time you create company loyalty (many employees see training as a reward or job perk).

Now you may be asking, "What if I find and train this person and they become a superstar and leave?"

Simple. Accept that some employees are going to leave, for whatever reason. You have the same risk with a mobile superstar. You just hire and start with someone new, but — and this is extremely important — you now have a system that identifies the appropriate KSA's for the role and you know the training required to groom the next person for greatness. You have also benefited from the time the employee worked for you while becoming a superstar in your system.

A workable system that can handle people leaving or be put into practice for future expansion is in place. You are not held hostage by the departure decisions of an individual. If you had hired only superstars, you would always start at square one after their departure.

If you handle all your critical employee positions (or just all positions) with this planned hiring and development approach based on KSA's, your business will continue successfully despite the inevitable threat of turnover. You may also develop a network of successful ex-employees who are indebted to you for the opportunity and training you provided. Since they know how your business works (using logical and planned processes), they may make future referrals or become clients themselves.

However, it may not even come to that, as properly training employees and ensuring continuing challenges will keep many loyal employees over any organization always looking to throw money at the next big hired gun.

Now that you are sold on finding good people who can develop, let's take a look at how to screen candidates to find the good ones to turn into homegrown superstars. This means critically analyzing candidates during the interview process.

Most importantly, forego typical interview questions that have nothing to do with your company's way of working or the position for which a candidate is applying. You want to determine if someone can accomplish the goals you have for the position.

Use open-ended questions pertaining to the type of work a candidate will be required to perform if hired. Ask them to explain how they would handle specific types of problems. Determine if their thought process is logical. Are they asking you the right questions to bound the problem and arrive at a reasonable solution? Ask the same questions in the same manner to all candidates to establish a basis for comparison.

Have more than one person interview a candidate to get a second opinion and also to determine how the candidate interacts with different personalities. Have individuals the new employee would interact with frequently ask their own questions. Make hiring a team approach so everyone has a vested interest in the success of the process.

When the interview is over, take stock of a candidate's professionalism. Good people don't switch these characteristics off and on. If they don't exhibit positive work traits when interviewing (when a good impression is most important), they probably won't change once they are on the job.

Did the candidate show up on time? Did they make a compelling case for being hired? Did they genuinely appear to want the position (did they ask for the job in their closing comments)? Did they show professional courtesy by sending thank you notes in a timely manner? Were their credentials and all communications spell checked and properly formatted? How did they treat other workers during the recruitment process? Was this person someone you would want interacting with clients (if applicable)?

Perform background checks on the people you hire, particularly for roles that require working with children, the infirm, financial records, security or interfacing with the public. Know who you are dealing with upfront to avoid potential legal violations or embarrassment later.

Check the candidate's references. Are they favorable and believable? Many former employers want to avoid possible legal difficulties, and as policy will only confirm previous employment and give dates of service. They will limit details, providing only vague but favorable comments. Approach references with the understanding that they are only a small part of the candidate's total professional picture, and their value may be minimal.

50

Find good candidates by networking through professional organizations in your industry. Go to events and speak with the leaders of such organizations; contact the editor of their internal trade publications and Web sites to advertise your needs.

Actively seek referrals from your current top performers. Good people tend to associate with other good people. Provide a cash bonus for accepted referrals from internal sources and have everyone's radar up.

Keep your eyes and ears open for talented individuals that contact your organization. A job-seeker who actively contacts your company and exhibits both an interest and knowledge of your business (evidenced through a well-written cover letter and follow-up phone conversation with astute and insightful questions) is likely more motivated to work for you than someone with whom you have to initiate contact.

Once you have hired someone, treat them right to promote growth so both they and your organization benefit. A little effort can make a huge difference in dealing with people.

Provide ongoing performance feedback and hold periodic reviews. Help key performers map out future goals and career paths in your organization — don't leave progress to chance. Determine what skills and internal assignments can get them to their goals.

Provide training that is timely, valuable and useful to an employee's current work or future development. Review compensation of all your positions to match the industry norm so coveted individuals have no reason to go elsewhere.

Lastly, provide sincere praise when it is earned and applicable. Many employees want to know they are contributing and making a positive difference. Sometimes a little recognition made in front of a worker's peers can be the best reward for a job well done.

More helpful hints on good hiring practices can be found online at:

- **www.inc.com/articles/2002/01/23815.html**
- **www.rbslaw.com/online_library_details.asp?id=49**

Alternatives to Direct Hiring

Sometimes there will be situations where it does not make business sense to hire a new employee to complete a project or assignment. You may be faced with a project of limited length, one requiring specialized skills or an initiative that is best viewed by an external source.

In these situations you may choose to enlist the aid of temporary workers or consultants.

Temporary (temp) workers or contract workers work for separate employment agencies that find assignments for them. A major advantage of this type of employee for the small business owner is the option to "try before you buy." If the temp doesn't work out, you can simply get a replacement. If the employee does turn out to be an asset you want to keep, you can usually negotiate with the person and their agency to hire them full-time.

Another advantage is that temp agencies, staffing firms and executive search firms have already screened candidates and performed their own background checks. It is usually faster to get someone in and working than it is through a direct hiring process.

The disadvantages are that many times people choose to be temps because they want a varied work environment and prefer not to stay in one company for an extended period of time. A well-qualified temp may also have multiple options for work assignments and you may not be their first choice when your firm's need arises.

For specific, well-defined projects or tasks that require business or technological expertise, consider business or professional consultants. Consultants work to complete a project under the terms of a mutually agreed upon contract. You do not directly control their activities (unless special provisions are included in the contract).

Consultants are generally considered to be highly skilled, and if procured from a large and well-established firm, are often highly educated with significant work experience.

The downside to using consultants is the expense. They are costly. Also, if changes to a project are required and are significant, renegotiations of contract terms may need to be worked out and work is usually delayed until the situation is resolved.

If you are a small contractor (in financial terms) for a larger consulting organization, you may not get the best and brightest, since those consultants are deployed to the larger revenue clients. If you use consultants, make sure the contract spells out the qualifications of the individuals working on the project and that substitutes must be approved by your management team.

* * *

Ask E-Diva

Dear E-Diva,

This is a new year. As a business owner, what type of resolutions should I be making for my company? I have some reservations on what we should be doing, but with your input maybe I can do the right things. Can you give me some suggestions or affirmations on this New Year?

Mr. Happy New Year Business Owner

Dear Mr. New Year,

Before I get started I would like to say happy New Year! You are starting off right by thinking about your business in a positive sense. Strategic planning is necessary in business, so a New Year's resolution for business is good business.

My suggestions are the following five high priority areas for improvement in 2005:

1. *HIRE AND TRAIN A GOOD TEAM: It's important to recruit and retain good team members who have the objective of supporting the business' interest. With that in mind, we as business owners need to invest dollars in supplying the training necessary in the areas of sales and business administration for the day to day of running the business. This may mean buying better equipment or software, etc.*

2. *ADVERTISEMENT: It's important and critical to understand your business' particular niche; it's equally imperative that you know your target market and, in turn, pin down the advertising media that best hits that segment. This year make sure every advertising dollar counts.*

3. *EXECELLENT CUSTOMER SERVICE: It's important to please the customer, whether current or prospective. This statement speaks for itself; however, troubleshooting any and all issues are vital to all businesses, so addressing the needs of the customer faster and better would be on the "A" list for 2005.*

4. *SHOW ME THE MONEY: It's important this year that you and your team follow the "Benjamin's." This may mean expanding your territory outside your current boundaries. New people, places, and things … lions, tigers and bears, OH MY! Much like in "The Wizard of Oz," this could mean a lot more travel, but life can be great outside of your home territory. Think about it!*

5. *DEVELOP THE LEADER WITHIN YOU: It's important for you as the business owner to*

continually get training for the development of your leadership skills. Inspiring others to do better can be a trip without the skills. Learn more about your craft and skill.

Remember: *Be a model that others can follow.*

E-Diva

* * *

Terminating Employment

Sometimes, despite your best efforts and due diligence during the hiring and training process, an employee who has been given ample opportunity does not work out as expected. Worse, they may have become a liability to your bottom line.

It may be time to terminate the employee agreement, or, more straightforwardly, fire the employee. This may sound cruel, but focus on the organizational perspective. You have made a conscious effort to hire performers with potential, trained them and provided the tools and support system to help them thrive. A poor performer at this point is diminishing the return of their fellow workers.

Additionally, considering the promise that exists within all of us, a poor performer is obviously not fulfilling their own potential given the present conditions. It may be in their best interest to pursue other avenues.

How do you go about firing someone once you've determined this is the best course of action for your organization? Well, the first step is not to make a rash decision. This means at the point where firing appears to be the best option, there should be a paper trail documenting a pattern of poor performance, violation of company policies or unethical business practices. There should also be documentation of the remediation methods that have been used to attempt to correct problems. This is typically the case with most well-run firms (provided we are not talking about immediate dismissal for egregious violations or outright illegal and dangerous activities).

Generally, the amount of time allotted for intervening attempts before firing will increase with the higher their level within the organization. This is not a hard and fast rule, but an hourly unskilled worker is generally easier to replace than an executive with broad supervisory responsibility or extensive project experience. The higher the level of someone within an organization, the higher the costs will be for hiring, training and compensating that person for the position. This leads many firms to try multiple means to salvage their investment in top-level employees.

The organization's termination process should be established and reviewed before you ever have to fire someone. The first step is always to check with your legal counsel to determine what constitutes the legal and illegal reasons for dismissing an employee.

The general rule of thumb is that an employee can be fired for a good reason or no reason at all. This last part is from the widely used at-will employment contract that specifies either party (employer or employee) can end the working relationship at any time. Good reasons (from the legal standpoint) for firing someone include incompetence, poor performance, excessive unexcused absences, sabotage, illegal activity or endangering the health and welfare of others.

Bad reasons for firings are any that are prohibited explicitly by applicable state or federal laws. Bad excuses can include dismissal of an employee for filing a workman's compensation claim, legally joining a union, being a member of a protected class or because the employee has testified about the company's illegal activities.

If you have business-oriented cause to fire someone and your decision is legal, you need to plan for the meeting with the employee. Prepare to perform the firing in a private place such as an enclosed office. Firing someone among a group of the person's peers can be demoralizing for everyone involved. You don't need to embarrass anyone.

Make arrangements to change or deny access to company computer systems, bank accounts, phone systems and other electronic or financial information that will go into effect immediately after the dismissal. Plan to collect security badges, keys, computers, cell phones, company car keys or any other company-owned property.

Inform building security that the individual will no longer be employed at the organization (after the date of the firing). Calculate any final compensation due to the employee and have a check ready for your meeting with them. Tell only those employees who need to know about the firing beforehand. You don't want to cause rumors or anxiety to spread and disrupt the office. Determine who needs to be present at the firing. Reasons for another person's presence are to serve as a witness or to explain evidence for the firing — such as documentation of warnings or poor performance evaluations. You may also need a human resources representative on hand to explain final compensation and continuation of health insurance.

If you feel the employee might pose a threat to others or themselves, you may need the assistance of security or a counselor. Try to limit the number of people present so as not to overwhelm the employee with an "us versus them" appearance. Aside from the witness or security, you can keep other essential staff on-call and have them enter and leave one at a time (if or as each becomes necessary).

Once you start the meeting with the employee, get to the point quickly. Tell the employee the legitimate legal reason for the firing and be firm in your position. Provide any necessary supporting evidence for your decision. By being straightforward and honest in dealing with the employee, you make it clear the firing decision will not be reversed. If you have methodically arrived at the decision to fire, you should not have doubts. Since the decision is clear, a professional business approach gives both parties the opportunity to make a clean break.

If after their dismissal the employee is calm, allow them to gather their items on their own and briefly say their goodbyes. If the employee shows significant signs of distress and the potential to hurt themselves or others, security will need to escort the individual to collect their items and leave.

If it is necessary to have the employee leave immediately, have their personal items delivered by mail. If you do mail items, use two employees to clean out possessions and ensure everything is shipped.

A decision to fire an employee is never easy, but if it must be done, most agree it should occur early in the week and fairly early in the day. This provides the ex-employee time to say goodbye to friends and leaves workdays during the remainder of the week for them to begin their job search and conduct other personal business.

The need to terminate employees can be difficult, especially when those being fired are well-liked or long-term employees. Two methods to assist the unemployed worker and demonstrate to remaining employees your compassion are to provide a severance check, job transition counseling or placement assistance.

The severance check sends a message that the company cares about the person's welfare and it may help pay their bills in the short-term. The employment resources assist the ex-employee to apply for unemployment and explore their future options.

Either one or both may serve to blunt any anger or bitterness the person harbors against your company.

55

Don't forget about the effect a firing has on the office work environment. Tell the remaining co-workers (those who need to be informed because they interacted or directly collaborated with the released employee) that their colleague was let go. There is no need to denigrate anyone's reputation or give negative details.

Let the remaining employees know the decision was made after thorough deliberation and with a focus on creating the best possible environment for the people present to best serve their customers. If you followed the advice I have given, this will be the case.

Negativity will only serve to drive down morale. Firing in a professional manner allows everyone to be treated with dignity and reflects well on your company.

More hints on good employee termination practices can be found online at:

- **http://www.wetfeet.com/employer/articles/article.asp?aid=389**
- **http://humanresources.about.com/od/discipline/a/fire_employee.htm**

SUMMARY

I know getting a business up and running takes significant effort. It puts tremendous demands on your time.

Be smart and delegate tasks and specialties to your core business team. Use your accountant to handle the day-to-day numbers and provide insightful tax and budgeting advice.

Hand off matters of legal consequence to your lawyer. Consult with experts in insurance to protect valuable assets.

Don't be afraid to get assistance with those areas you have little experience (such as marketing, finance, operations or public relations). Utilize supplemental sources such as nationally-recognized small business organizations, higher education institutions and the Internet to bolster your understanding and to familiarize yourself with industry best practices. Taking a team approach to tackling business challenges does not diminish your role and responsibility as a leader, but instead works to augment your decision-making process.

Make your internal teams more effective by putting your top talent on the most important projects. Provide teams with clear business goals. Give them ownership of successful completion of goals.

Have management increase efficiency by eliminating obstacles to progress, providing the necessary tools to complete tasks and utilizing continual feedback. After a project is complete, capture best practices learned and have members evaluate and constructively critique everyone's performances so they may keep improving.

After all, if your team keeps improving, so will your bottom line.

E-Diva
Dr. Rae Pearson

Chapter Five

Finding and Keeping the Best Employees

" Nothing is an obstacle unless you say it is."
– Wally Amos, founder of Famous Amos Cookies

Ask any leader what the hardest part of running a business is and she'll probably tell you it is finding, hiring, and keeping employees.

If done well, your employees can be the ultimate ambassadors for your company. They can motivate their colleagues and surpass customer expectations. They can keep you efficient so your profits are high and your headaches are minimal.

Done poorly, however, hiring can bring you and other employees down. It can slow production, lower morale, and cause countless mistakes in the workplace.

All of which can cost you in time, money, and reputation.

That's why I've always emphasized knowing how to hire and retain the best people. In fact, research shows that well-selected employees who feel respected and appreciated are more productive, have fewer sick days and are less likely to create conflicts.

While it can be difficult to identify the right people (given the short time frame and limited resources associated with the typical hiring process), it is possible to weed out the wrong ones. Lord knows I've had to learn how to separate the wheat from the chaff.

So let's get rolling. In this chapter, I'll provide you with some tips for hiring the best candidates, developing policies that will help you keep them and knowing when it's time to say goodbye before a bad hire can hurt you.

WHO ARE YOU LOOKING FOR?

When it comes to hiring employees, I've learned there's nothing mysterious about the process. It's been the same for as long as most of us can recall — we post a job ad, pore through resumes, interview candidates, cross our fingers, and make an offer.

YOU CAN'T ASK THAT: Application and Interview Pitfalls

To hire a candidate, you need to ask a lot of questions. If you don't know which questions are okay and which aren't, however, you could be heading into a potential landmine — where even the most innocent step can cost you money and even your job. I recommend the following guidelines:

• **Make sure every question you ask relates to an applicant's ability to do the job.** Stick to questions that directly related to the position.

• **Exclude any questions about race and ethnicity.** Don't request a photograph or ask about an applicant's eye or hair color or social affiliations on a job application.

• **Don't ask about their national origin.** While you can ask if they're eligible to work in America, you can't ask about an applicant's birthplace, social security number (until an offer is made) or proficiency in English, (unless it's a bona fide job requirement).

• **The American with Disabilities Act (ADA) prohibits you from asking about a person's medical history.** That includes sick days, workers compensation injuries or claims, mental health problems or past addiction to drugs prior to being hired. You can, however, ask about the candidate's current situation.

• **Don't ask about a person's maiden name, gender, or marital status.** That includes family plans, childcare arrangements, and title preferences (Ms., Mrs., or Miss). You can ask if an applicant has ever been known by another name to facilitate accurate background checks.

• **Verify whether an applicant is of legal age to work.** But don't ask for an age, date of birth or information such as graduation dates (unless you need that information for the job).

Some other no-no's, unless directly related to the job, include questions about religion, union membership, military status, criminal record, finances, legal off-duty activities (like smoking and drinking), and sexual orientation.

As a further precaution, it's good practice to include an equal employment opportunity statement on your application that states you do not discriminate against applicants based on membership in a protected class.

It's a simple program that all too often doesn't, but should, start with a clear idea of the type of person you're looking for. Unfortunately, too many hiring managers reach out for resumes prematurely, asking questions, calling references, and making decisions that, all too often, turn out to be the wrong ones.

That's because if you climb into a haystack looking for needle when what you really need is a rubber band, you may be setting yourself up for disappointment.

Instead, before you place a want ad or get as far as the first interview, I recommend writing down exactly what you want in a new employee, both in terms of experience, skills, personality, and work ethic. This will help you weed out those people who don't fit into the picture of what you (and your team, if appropriate) have decided the position calls for.

As you think about the right hire's credentials, be specific. Think about personality traits and relationship skills. Review the exact position and identify exactly what it needs and how you'll evaluate for it. Ask yourself, for example, if you want somebody who:

- Is looking for a short- or long-term opportunity?
- Is friendly under stress?
- Is outgoing or quiet (if you need a marketer to staff an exhibit booth, you may want somebody who's more outgoing).
- Can build a team or consensus among business leaders or work individually?
- Prefers details or big pictures?
- Is a lone ranger or a team player?
- Is proactive or reactive?
- Prefers structure or ambiguity?

You should also decide at this time whether you want prospects to sign a non-compete agreement, which is especially important for people in jobs that interact with proprietary information; or go through pre-employment drug testing and medical screening.

These are all important questions to answer before you draft the job description. Once you have the answers, you'll be well-prepared to craft something accurate, put out your feelers, and draw the right types of people — and resumes — to your company.

Which leads me to my next point: When you finally do get a resume, take the time to read it.

All too often, hiring managers get resumes and fail to read through them in their entirety. They skim through the beginning and scan the rest quickly.

A resume is not the *Wall Street Journal*, where reading just the front page is often enough to give you all the pertinent information. To the contrary, a resume is designed to be read for maximum impact. That's the best and only way to identify, at least initially, a person's education, job history, skills and interests — as well as any red flags, like gaps in employment, job hopping, or an inappropriate presentation.

HOW TO GET THE MOST AUTHENTIC INTERVIEW

Once you've outlined the job, waded through resumes and come up with three to five potential candidates, it's time to meet them in person in an interview setting.

I always recommend conducting at least two interviews with a candidate before hiring him or her, especially if the position is higher level (leadership, executive, etc.). Often, in the second interview, a candidate will let his guard down, giving you a chance to meet the real person (in fact, you'll frequently get an entirely different impression when you meet someone for the second time).

In both meetings, you should make candidates feel welcome and put them at ease. That's because relaxed applicants give more complete answers to your questions, helping you better judge whether they're right for the job (and your company).

I also recommend having at least two people interview the final candidates, because the hiring process is highly subjective. You'll get the best outcome by involving as many people and perspectives as appropriate.

PREPARE A STRONG LIST OF QUESTIONS

As you prepare for the interview, take a good amount of time to think about and create a strong list of questions — both specific (based on the applicant's resume) and general (based on their history, experience, and skills) — to use when interviewing multiple candidates.

Some good questions to ask are what the potential employee believes his or her greatest asset is; what their favorite tasks are and why; what they would do in certain job-related situations; how they would prevent certain mishaps or inefficiencies; and why they liked or did not like working for the last company they were employed by.

What you don't want to do is ask about somebody's personal life, since that could get you into trouble. Instead, keep it relevant. Probe around legitimate issues; those related to each candidate's ability to perform on the job. Be clear in what you're asking and give people enough time to respond. Ask the same questions of each prospect in the same way so you can fairly and accurately compare their responses.

Remember, applicants are also assessing you. Put your best foot forward, and promote your company as a good place to work.

At the end of the interview, tell the candidate what the next steps are and when they might expect to hear something. Don't jump the gun and make it seem like a candidate already has the job. You may meet somebody you think is great in the moment, and that's fine, but this is not the place to be spontaneous. Choosing the right person requires a certain amount of time spent weighing and evaluating your options.

WHAT TO DO AFTER THE INTERVIEW

You've interviewed your top candidates twice and now you have to make an offer. That triggers the next step in the process, which includes checking references and deciding who, of all the candidates you interviewed, would be the best asset to the job and your organization.

When it comes to checking references, I always recommend using what you learn as just another piece of information about the candidate in question.

While hearing from other employers can be helpful, you don't want to put too much weight on it, because you simply don't know what their motivation is in giving positive feedback about the candidate. Sometimes, they do it in fear legal action or want to get the candidate off their unemployment. Many employers will only verify only a previous employee's position and employment dates, because they are worried about potential defamation claims.

Consider references to be part of the bigger picture in learning about how well-suited prospects might be to your company.

Once you've spoken to all references, compare notes. Think about the interview itself and imagine each applicant at work doing the job. How do they look in your mind? Were they articulate and professional? Do they have the skills, education, experience, and personality traits that are required?

Are they too focused on money (be careful if the answer is yes, as this may carry over into the job), or are they enthusiastic about what they bring to the table and the idea of growing professionally?

As you consider the answers to these questions and the information you've gathered, don't be fooled by a polished or pumped-up resume or a smooth talker. Some people are great job hunters because they can't hold one.

ONCE YOU'VE GOT THEM, KNOW HOW TO KEEP THEM

Once you've hired the right employee, it's your job to keep them. That means providing the support system necessary to help them succeed and thrive.

I'm not suggesting you eliminate the need for personal accountability; if you've hired well, you've already got somebody who takes pride in the quality of their work and professionalism.

What I am saying is that right kinds of leadership, involvement, and company policies go a long way in avoiding the high costs (like low morale, customer dissatisfaction, and inefficiencies) associated with excessive turnover and recruitment.

Following is some advice for making sure the people you hire stay with .

Be a good leader. Personal charisma and the ability to inspire are vital executive qualities. If you cannot inspire employees with your dynamic leadership and vision, at least avoid trying to motivate them with threats.

Too many managers either over-control or under-control their people; they're either micromanagers or macro-managers. Instead, be a supportive manager. Give them the tools and guidance necessary to do what's required; let them accomplish their jobs independently.

Manage for results, not for process. Learn to listen and respond to their needs. If you do that, your employees will want to work hard for you (I've seen it time and time again). It'll be a win-win situation.

Develop initiatives and policies that involve and inspire employees. The best way to ensure people will stay with you through the constant change that's part of business is to involve them in important decisions and company policies. And don't forget to inspire them.

Many employees leave their jobs because they feel underappreciated or bored. You can prevent that by:

GETTING THE MOST FROM A REFERENCE

Here are some tips for making that call to a reference count.

• **Use reference experts.** Get either an internal expert (human resource professional) on the topic or contract the job out to consultants or recruiting agencies with expertise.

• **Get specific information.** Ask the candidate to give examples of past work performance with previous employers. Make it clear you will verify this information, and then use the material to formulate your questions to ask the previous employer.

• **Obtain written releases to contact former employers.** Have the form release both you and the former employers from any legal liability based on information obtained during the check.

• **Verify prior employment status and salary information.** Make sure your candidate did, indeed, work for the contact given as the former employer. Request a base salary history and any additional compensation as reported on the W-2 form.

• **Build rapport.** Prior to a telephone contact, fax or mail the candidate's written waiver and authorization to conduct the check. Give your name, position, and telephone number, and emphasize you only want job-related information about the candidate.

• **Ask targeted questions.** Frame questions based on specific examples the candidate provided in the interview process. For example: "This candidate stated she was the design engineer on a project that netted the company $100,000 profit. Can you verify her function and tell me her contributions to the project?"

• **Document all reference responses.** Keep an accurate, written record of all the reference discussions to support your hiring decisions. Protect the confidentiality of the information you uncover, disclosing only to people within your organization who need to be involved.

REJECTING JOB APPLICANTS

What do you tell the candidates to whom you didn't extend a job offer?

By law, you don't have to tell them anything. In fact, most legal experts will advise you to provide as little information as possible. Telling them they simply don't have the qualifications necessary is enough.

But there may be those instances when you want to provide applicants with a more detailed explanation (either they've been in for several interviews or are applying for a position in leadership). In that case:

• Explain, in an honest and succinct way, the legitimate, business-related reasons for the rejection.

• Help the candidate improve by telling him about any deficiencies in his interviewing skills. For example, if he's qualified on paper but has trouble providing real-life examples of his abilities in person, he should work on his presentation.

• Don't be bullied into giving more information than you're comfortable with. If the candidate pushes for or threatens to take legal action, end the conversation and thank him for his time.

• Promoting and rewarding high (yet achievable) performance objectives.

• Providing ways to achieve personal goals inside the organization.

• Enabling executives, managers, and supervisors to develop professionally.

• Providing abundant opportunities for promotion from within — and being vocal about them with employees.

• Supporting employees in getting the training they need, especially when it comes to understanding and implementing company policies.

• Communicating the organization's vision, values, and expectations frequently and creatively.

• Involving employees in controlling costs by soliciting their ideas and input and keeping them informed every step of the way.

You could also try practicing what I call "guerilla inspiration." That means closing the office for an hour one morning to watch funny videos, announcing occasional half day vacations, or arranging donuts and videos for employees on random afternoons.

Have a system for appraising employee performance regularly. If you're not reviewing your employees' performance each year, you may be missing the chance to improve employee relations, satisfaction, and productivity, because a performance evaluation can be an effective retention tool. Most employees want and need constructive feedback on how they're doing.

But a yearly review, as is typical in most organizations, doesn't always cut it. That's because annual appraisals tend to focus on things that have already happened. Instead, I recommend giving your employees regular, ongoing evaluations and structured guidance to help them both set and achieve job and career objectives.

That means:

- Giving informal feedback every day, focusing on performance objectives rather than past mistakes or failures. This requires you to watch your employees regularly and work closely with them.

- Working with your employees to set short- and long-term performance goals, based on an identified combination of job responsibilities, core competencies, and future aspirations. Make sure they're specific and measurable.

- Developing action plans to help you work with an employee who is having performance problems. Use these plans to identify and discuss problems with employees as they happen and suggest improvements. Then update and revisit them regularly to detail problems and solutions and make sure they're being implemented successfully.

- Conducting formal reviews that document the "big picture" of an employee's performance and career. Ideally, these should be done several times a year. This is not the time to talk about performance problems (you should already be doing that); but rather to assess whether the employee has met his goals and is following the right path for developing his career.

DO YOU NEED WRITTEN POLICIES?

When was the last time you reviewed your organization's policies? If you're like many employers, this is at the bottom of a lengthy to-do list.

Having well-written policies — those that are carefully developed, updated, and used — can serve as an effective communication device and help you stay out of court.

A policies and procedures manual should:

- Guide both managers and employees as to what is expected and can prevent misunderstandings.

- Support supervisors and managers in consistently applying clearly communicated policies.

- Be used to illustrate your commitment to a positive work environment and nondiscriminatory employment practices.

Here are some commonly-asked question and answers about written policies.

ARE ALL EMPLOYERS REQUIRED TO HAVE WRITTEN POLICIES?

Not by law, but it's a good idea in terms of helping you establish good faith compliance with federal and state courts, especially when it comes to hotbed issues like sexual harassment, equal opportunity and the Family and Medical Leave Act.

DOES EVERY ORGANIZATION NEED WRITTEN POLICIES?

As a general rule, every employer, except maybe those with fewer than 15 employees, should have written policies. Employers with 15 or more employees are covered by federal discrimination laws (such as Title VII and the Americans with Disabilities Act) and most state discrimination laws.

Written policies are a good starting point to show your commitment to nondiscriminatory employment practices. For example, a performance review policy can show the job-related criteria used to evaluate employees and any safeguards used to ensure the process is conducted fairly and objectively.

Smaller employers should at least consider creating a handbook since it is likely they already have some policies in writing. For example, employment offer letters may explain vacation and sick leave accrual while other items, like a posted memo, may outline pay procedures.

DO WE RISK CREATING A CONTRACT IF WE HAVE WRITTEN POLICIES?

The simple act of putting your policies in writing should not create a binding contract, especially if the policies are written as guidelines that explain what your general requirements are and how employees will be treated.

That said, it's important to build flexibility into your wording (using terms like "generally," "typically," "usually" and "may") and steer clear of any promises that could be interpreted as a contract. For example, don't:

- State that the organization will "only" or "always" do something or "must" act in a particular way.
- Describe employees as permanent.
- Make promises of job security.

WHAT IS THE DIFFERENCE BETWEEN A SUPERVISORY POLICY MANUAL AND AN EMPLOYEE HANDBOOK?

A supervisory policy manual is generally intended as a guide for managers and supervisors so they have a reference to make sure the organization's policies are being implemented; an employee handbook is designed to provide general information about the organization's practices, benefits, work hours, pay policies, and work rules to employees. It usually does not include information about supervisory procedures.

It's a good idea to have both.

WHAT POLICIES SHOULD WE INCLUDE?

In choosing policies to include, you should consider:

- Your culture and any recurring issues or problems.

- Any memos on policy topics (such as vacation and holiday schedules) and past practices.
- The standard in human resource practices for your industry.

Most employers also include information about pay, benefits, breaks, personal conduct, attendance, harassment issues, equal employment opportunity, disciplinary procedures, termination, performance appraisals, smoking, safety procedures, appropriate dress and appearance, use of communications systems (such as the telephone and Internet) and drug and alcohol use.

IS THE JOB EVER DONE?

No, because your policies should be dynamic and change along with the company. You may need to add to them, revise them or even delete them. You'll also need your legal counsel to review them, as state and federal laws can change rapidly.

WHEN AN EMPLOYEE NEEDS TO BE FIRED

While you can do everything right as a leader — implement the right policies, provide the support and tools necessary to enable job success, and work with an employee on an action plan to minimize problems — you still may have to let somebody go.

It's best to make the conversation short and be direct, clearly stating the reason for the termination. Show the person courtesy by giving him an opportunity to gather his bearings and belongings and say goodbye to his co-workers. Show sympathy.

65

There's really no magic bullet for this one. Often, it's simply a matter of taking a deep breath and remembering that you've done all you can in terms of guiding this person. Now it's time to wish them well in their next endeavor.

After they leave, it helps to review the characteristics that drew you to that hire in the first place and re-evaluate so you don't make the same mistake again as you look for his replacement.

AVOIDING LEGAL PROBLEMS DURING LAYOFFS

A layoff is the temporary or permanent elimination of jobs for business-related reasons. It focuses more on an overall reduction in force rather than an individual in a targeted position.

While nobody wants to go through a layoff, often it's the only viable option for companies going through a downturn in business or a realignment of priorities. Often it's very emotional.

For employers, however, the potential impact can also be costly in generating employment discrimination claims. These are claims that typically result from disproportionately laying off employees who:

- Are protected class members (for example, because they are minorities, female, or disabled).

- Are older and tend to be more highly compensated and may be selected because of their higher salaries.
- Have engaged in legally protected activities, such as filing workers' compensation claims or engaging in union activity.

To limit these claims, your best defense is to be able to demonstrate the following business-related and job-related reasons for layoff decisions:

Length of service. This is based on fairness and ease of implementation. Also, many union contracts require seniority to be a primary consideration in determining layoffs.

Performance. That means laying off unproductive, mediocre, or problem employees first. Use this system fairly so it accurately reflects employee job performance. If evaluations are biased or conducted carelessly, layoff decisions can impact women and minorities, for example, which could lead to discrimination claims.

Job skills. This requires the skills, knowledge, and training for each employee be accurately documented and properly used for job decisions.

Job elimination. Layoffs are based on an assessment of the relative value of particular positions. This approach does not require the employer to make personal assessments and tends to carry less of a stigma for the affected employee.

Voluntary layoff incentives. Some employers offer incentives, such as severance pay and continued health insurance, to entice employees to volunteer to be laid off. While this approach allows employees to choose their exit, it also puts you at risk of losing your best employees.

Finally, some employers choose to offer severance to laid-off employees, but it's not mandated by law. Depending on your location, you may have to pay employees for unused vacation time.

If you have 20 or more employees and provide a group health plan, you must offer workers the opportunity to continue coverage under the Consolidated Omnibus Budget Reconciliation Act (COBRA), at their own expense, for up to 18 months.

While hiring, retaining, and firing employees can be challenging, it can also be rewarding. Watching your business grow as a result of developing the right corporate team and culture is one of the highlights of being an entrepreneur.

Understanding how to find and inspire people — and to build the foundation that ensures their success and yours — is one of the most vital components of building a strong business that will endure.

* * *

Ask E-Diva

Dear E-Diva,

My business is growing and I would like to hire more employees. Which laws apply for my business growth?

Mr. Growing Businessman

Dear Mr. Growing Businessman,

Congratulations! As a business grows and more employees are hired, your responsibilities will increase with more regulations and laws. However, even having one employee requires compliance.

I would suggest you hire a human resource firm or employ an experienced human resource manager to keep you out of trouble. The following are some basic federal laws and regulations with the employee level for compliance by employers in most general industries:

For one or more employees

- *Federal and state payroll withholding regulation*
- *IRS withholding, FICA (Social Security) Withholding, Medicare withholding, garnishments and wage liens, child support withholding*
- *Federal and state wage and hour laws*
- *Fair Labor Standards Act (FLSA: Specifies wages, hours, acceptable working conditions, record keeping requirements and regulations for employment of minors.*
- *Equal Pay Act of 1963: Requires equal pay for equal work, prohibits discrimination in pay based on gender.*
- *National Labor Relations Act (NLRA): Gives employees the right to organize, join unions and engage in collective bargaining, protects against unfair labor practices.*
- *Employee Retirement Income Security Act of 1974 (ERISA): Regulates pension and retirement plans, regulates welfare benefits plans (health and life insurance).*
- *Health Insurance Portability and Accountability Act of 1996 (HIPAA): Covers any employer that offers health coverage to employees; requires disclosure notices and certificates of coverage when employee's coverage ends.*

- *Immigration Reform and Control Act of 1986:-Requires employers to verify identity and employment eligibility for people hired after November 6, 1986 (Form I-9),requires workplace poster*

- *Occupational Safety and Health Act of 1970 (OSHA):Federal law that may be enforced by state law whose regulations equal or exceed federal requirements; requires workplaces be free of hazards that may cause death or serious physical harm, requires workplace poster.*

- *Employee Polygraph Protection Act of 1988: Generally prohibits use of polygraph and lie detectors by employers, requires workplace poster.*

- *Rehabilitation Act of 1973: Covers employers with federal government contracts of $2,500 or more or who receive federal financial assistance; requires employers to reasonably accommodate disabled employees and job applicants.*

- *Uniformed Services Employment and Re-employment Rights Act of 1994: Guarantees re-employment rights to employees after military service requires that employers do not discriminate against employees for activities required by service in the military, State National Guard or uniformed civilian service.*

- *Consumer Credit Protection Act: Prohibits employers from discharging an employee because of garnishment of wages.*

- *The Fair Credit Reporting Act: Requires employers who reject job applicants because of written credit reports to give applicant notice and supply name and address of credit reporting agency issuing the report.*

- *Whistle Blower Laws: Protect employees from retaliation for reporting violations by employers of certain safety and/or environmental standards.*

- *Personal Responsibility and Work Opportunity Reconciliation Act of 1996: Requires all employers to submit information about every new hire within 20 days of hire; each state designates appropriate agency to receive the information.*

- *Omnibus Transportation Employee Testing Act: Requires employers in the transportation industry (FHWA, FRA, FTA, FAA, and RSPA) to implement alcohol and drug testing programs, maintain records related to testing and provide drug and alcohol education to employees.*

For four or more employees

- *Immigration Reform and Control Act of 1986: Protects against discrimination based on national origin.*

For 15 or more employees

- *Title VII of the Civil Rights Act of 1964: Requires equal employment opportunity, protects against discrimination based on race, color, religion, sex and national origin, protects against sexual harassment in the workplace; requires workplace poster.*

- *Pregnancy Discrimination Act of 1978: Defines pregnancy as a temporary disability and requires accommodation on the job, guarantees right to return to same or similar job with same pay following the disability.*

- *Drug-Free Workplace Act of 1988: Requires federal contractors with contracts of $100,000 or more to maintain drug-free workplaces and follow specific regulations involving drug-testing and employee notification, requires random drug testing for federal workers holding sensitive jobs, requires testing in certain employees regulated by the U.S. Department of Transportation.*

- *Americans with Disabilities Act of 1990: Provides protection in employment for people who are physically or mentally disabled, requires reasonable accommodation for those otherwise qualified to perform essential job functions; requires workplace poster.*

- *Civil Rights Act of 1991: Allows jury trials for employment discrimination cases, sets limits on punitive damage awards, establishes employer requirements for defense.*

For 20 or more employees

- *Age Discrimination in Employment Act of 1967 (ADEA): Protects against discrimination in employment for employees who are at least 40 years of age.*

- *Consolidated Omnibus Budget Reconciliation Act of 1986 (COBRA):Requires employers who provide certain benefit programs to offer continuation coverage to former employees and their dependents; employer may bill cost to former employee along with administrative fee of up to 2% of the cost.*

For 50 or more employees

- *Family and Medical Leave Act (FMLA): Allows employees with more than one year of service to be eligible for up to 12 weeks unpaid leave in a 12-month period after childbirth or adoption, to care for a seriously ill child, spouse or parent, or for the employee's own serious illness, requires employers to continue to pay for benefit coverage for employees on FMLA leave; guarantees return to work for same or similar job at same pay, prohibits discrimination against anyone exercising these provisions; enforced by the U.S. Equal Employment Opportunity Commission (EEOC).*

- *Executive Order 11246 – Affirmative Action: Requires a written Affirmative Action Plan (AAP) for minorities and women by federal contractors with $50,000 or more in contracts and 50 or more employees; all federal funds depositories (i.e. banks); and all paying agents for U.S. savings bonds, requires goals and timetables for elimination of underutilization of minorities and females in any job group (federal contractors with contracts or subcontracts valued at $10,000 or more in 12 months, must have a written AAP for disabled and veterans).*

For 100 or more employees

- *Workers Adjustment and Retraining Notification Act of 1988 (WARN): Requires employers to provide 60 days' notice to employees of plant closing or mass layoffs (employment loss of 50 or more people, excluding part-time workers), requires notification of public officials in surrounding communities.*

- *Equal Employment Opportunity Commission Regulations (EEOC): Requires employers of 100 or more and all federal government contractors and subcontractors who* *have both a contract of $50,000 or more and 50 or more employees to file a Standard Form 100 report by September 30 of each year showing sex and ethnic breakdown of workforce statistics within EEO job categories; additional detailed reports of distribution by compensation are required of some employers.*

Mr. Growing Businessman, this information is only intended as a summary of federal laws and regulations applying to employers. This is not legal advice. Many states enact laws to supplement or expand upon federal legislation and many enact laws particular to employers in that state only. In addition to the federal regulations, all employers should carefully research the laws applicable to the state in which the business is located.

E-Diva

* * *

Chapter Six

Managing Employees: Keeping Politics Out of the Office

" For most people, it's not what they are that holds them back, it's what they think they are not."

– John C. Maxwell, author, minister and motivational speaker

I recently read a great quote from author Mark Twain on motivation – the key element, in my opinion, of managing employees.

"Keep away from people who try to belittle your ambitions," said Twain. "Small people always do that, but the really great make you feel that you, too, can become great."

I've been running my own business for over two decades, and it honestly didn't take me long to realize you can't motivate people with negatives.

I remember a sales professional I knew who was pretty good at closing deals, but not so good once he was promoted into management. This guy would read his sales staff the riot act after a particularly disappointing quarter.

The more he hammered away on their supposed flaws and failures, the more resentment he created among the sales force. The more he railed at his staff, the more the room filled with tension and anxiety.

You could actually feel the motivation draining away, like air leaving a deflating balloon.

I felt bad for the sales employees, and I felt disgusted with the sales manager. He didn't know what I and other experienced business owners already knew: Your company is only as good as the people who work with you.

Treating people decently isn't just the decent thing to do (although it is the right thing to do). It's also good business. Business owners who disrespect and devalue their employees risk missing out on big-time savings and profits.

Gallup International says businesses in the top 24% of employee engagement have less turnover and remarkably higher percentages of customer loyalty, profitability and revenues. Another report from the Hay Group uncovered powerful links between employee

What Employees Want from You as a Leader

• To trust you and for you to trust them. Begin by being trustworthy and extending trust.

• Good two-way communication. Begin by being a good listener.

• To be challenged. Set forth your vision and goals clearly and then let your workers exercise their creativity and authority in meeting your goals.

• Accountability. Not only should you hold them accountable for their own performance, but you should measure your own performance as well.

• Recognition. Offer praise and express appreciation at every opportunity.

Tips on Employee Performance Reviews

• Concentrate on what you and the employee can achieve together in the future. Don't use performance reviews just as a means of telling workers about everything they're doing wrong.

• Strive for consistency and fairness. Apply performance criteria to all employees, not just a few.

• Encourage employees to evaluate themselves and to discuss their own strengths. Your view of an employee and the employee's view of himself should match fairly well. Otherwise, it's a warning signal.

• Be honest about poor performance, but not brutal. Document your observations in writing.

• If you're small enough that constant communication and feedback are taking place, you may be able to avoid performance reviews. But don't send the message that performance isn't critical.

Helping Employees Take Pride in Their Work

• Employees are your most important assets, so hire the best, provide training and growth opportunities, and recognize good performance.

• Have a meaningful, concise and realistic job description for each employee. Make sure you review it with the employee and that it is understood.

• Be sure employees know what is expected of them. Establish high standards of performance ethics.

• Offer specialized training or skills enhancement to your current employees. Promoting from within encourages and motivates your greatest assets—your current workforce.

• Create a new employee referral bonus program. Describe your needs in title and duties and offer a reward for your most wanted.

Promoting From Within

• Understand your advantage. In a small company, you are in a better position to know what people's abilities and interests are than in a large company.

• Develop a nose for hidden talent. Find out what skills people use when they're not at work and determine if those skills can be put to use in your company – in a higher position.

• Create career paths for employees. Your people need opportunities to grow.

• Consider the work you outsource. Can that work be brought inside, creating an advancement opportunity for one of your employees?

• If an employee needs outside training for a higher-level job, pay for it. That will be cheaper than recruiting a new employee.

Hands-On Leadership

• Be there. Entrepreneurs warn that a successful business can slip when an owner is not there at least part of every day, keeping in touch with how things are going.

• Set an example for working hard. One wholesale bakery owner sometimes sleeps on the couch in his office so he can be there when the early shift comes in at 4 a.m.

• Don't confuse "hands-on" managing with micromanagement. Set objectives and offer guidance, but don't make employees do every little thing your way. Gauge what they do by the results.

• Understand your business down to the last detail. The founder of a toy store chain visits the stores and spends time doing each job (selling, clerking, etc.) and observing customers' reactions.

• Stay in touch with "stakeholders" – including customers, employees and suppliers.

72

Cultivating Confident Employees

• Ask them to be responsible for progressively larger projects.

• Use them as examples (in their presence) when describing to others how to do something.

• Give them feedback at various times during a project – not just at its completion.

• Send a note of praise to them or better still, to their direct boss.

• Ask for their opinions and advice on matters not necessarily related to their normal duties.

Creating an Innovative Environment

• Show your employees that you think of innovation as an ongoing process. Some ideas will work and many won't. Keep experimenting.

• Listen, listen, listen. Innovation is a collaborative process.

• Be open to "accidents" – the unexpected connections that spark new ideas. Inspiration comes from everywhere, often from outside your own field.

• Draw on your own employees – they know the company's problems and goals best. This is probably one time you don't need outside consultants.

• Be patient. Creativity can't be hurried.

engagement and productivity, which ultimately impacts the bottom line.

A key 2002 report from the consulting firm Watson Wyatt Worldwide, soundly confirms that happy and motivated employees contribute to a company's bottom line. The study says if a company makes a "significant improvement" in key pay and benefits practices, its market value will rise 16.5 %.

The Wyatt study confirms the findings of another study on the impact of employees' degree of happiness and well-being from the State University of New York at Buffalo's School of Management. In five annual surveys that polled 3,000 companies, the SUNY study found significant jumps in an index of human-capital improvements tend to lift shareholder value 20%.

73

GETTING PEOPLE MOTIVATED THE E-DIVA WAY

You can make and save money by keeping employees engaged and eager to see the company succeed.

The clearest and most effective way to get to that cherished landmark is to apply the Golden Rule and treat people like you want to be treated. Remember earlier in this chapter when I was discussing my relationship with employees? Notice when I talked about employees, I said "working with you" and not "working for you."

Sure, I pay the bills and make the decisions but I'm smart enough to know I can't pull off the successful operation of my business by walking around lording my "boss status" over the staff.

That doesn't work and doesn't appeal to me on any level. That's why I prefer the phrase "working with people."

How does this apply to managing your staff and making the most of employees? At the end of this chapter, if I accomplish anything, I want it to be getting the point across that the employer-employee relationship has to be a "win-win" to succeed. The elements of win-win are things like trust, respect, honesty, commitment and the shared acknowledgement that you can't win unless you put the "real" boss first: The customer.

Not everyone you hire will buy into that mindset. For whatever reason, you will encounter flagging enthusiasm, stubbornness, know-it-alls or that whirlwind you hired six months ago who isn't buying into your vision for your business or the path you've chosen to get there.

It's tempting in such situations, to throw your hands in the air and utter the worst five words an entrepreneur can say . . . "I will do it myself."

Other variations on that phrase include:

- "I don't need help. I'll remember it when I talk to the client."
- "I don't know what to delegate."
- "I can't afford to hire anyone."
- "I'm too critical of other people's work."
- "If I give up control over everything, things will start to fall through the cracks."

74

Even if you do have an unmotivated staffer or two (and you will), you can't afford to take the responsibility of running your own business and place it on your shoulders.

It is much better, in my experience, to take concrete steps to motivate your employees and have them do it. After all, you're a business owner with a lot on your plate already.

That's why delegating is so important. And you can't delegate if you can't motivate.

All the key ingredients in the delegating cake – knowing what to do and what to delegate, creating a plan, good hiring practices, holding people accountable, and following up with staffers – won't amount to much if you can't get people to buy in to what you are doing.

The best way to accomplish that – surprise, surprise – is through good communication. I've learned a few things in this area, so let me share them with you.

Set the tone ... and get out of the way. As I've been saying in these pages all along, the best way to learn is by trial and error. You learn by doing, by making mistakes and by learning from them.

Make it face-to-face. I know a lot of business owners who think they can manage people by e-mail or cell phone.

Or worse, by memo.

Hey, technology is great, but the next manager I meet who can motivate an employee on a Blackberry will be the first one. Here's my rule of thumb: You wouldn't consider trying to motivate a customer to buy from you strictly by e-mail or by phone. Ideally, you'd meet them face-to-face. Why should managing employees be any different? Looking people in the eye is always the best way to interact with them.

Be crystal clear. I've made the critical mistake over the years of assuming that everyone else understands the issues of the day just as well as I do.

Not so – and it was mostly my fault.

Just because I've made my life's mission – career-wise, anyway – knowing the intricacies of my business doesn't mean my employees have done the same. So instead of wasting time telling people what to do, make sure they know what to do by asking questions like "what steps will you take to get the job done here?" or "what do you need to know from me?"

Keep it positive, and keep the personal out of it. Who wants to be jawboned into submission by a territorial tyrant who likes to see folks squirm? Not me, although I know plenty of despots and bullies (but I don't know too many who remain successful).

My take is different. Instead of relying on withering criticism to make a point, I prefer to accentuate the positive and handle even flops and failures as a learning experience. If you keep the personal out of it and treat people with respect, they'll run through walls for you (metaphorically, of course).

The crazy thing is, in my experience, so many employees have been beaten down before they come to me that they just about expect to be bullied and mistreated. What a shame – but what a wonderful opportunity to show them a better way, and help your company by leaps and bounds in the process.

Have the patience of a saint. God knows a business owner has eight million things to do and that time is the biggest commodity of all. But I've found you can use time to your advantage when dealing with employees. I like to schedule one-on-ones and give employees my undivided attention.

Sure, that takes time. But a little time now saves a lot of time later. And giving folks your undivided attention makes them feel like a key ingredient in your business (because they are).

Listen up. When you're making time to be with employees, elicit comments and draw them out. These people are on the front lines and know what's going on. You'd be crazy not to listen to them.

Let me amend that – you'd be crazy not to listen *closely* to them.

Be a good sounding board. People appreciate hearing from you. The good ones do, anyway.

Learning from you is like going back to school. A lot of your employees want to get ahead and information from the business owner … no schooling could be more valuable than that.

Go ahead and give employees feedback – and not just during annual reviews. Historically, employees crave improvement. They want to get better. To them, valuable feedback is manna from heaven.

Always, always be positive. Let go of any negative opinions you may have about your employees. Approach each of them as a source of unique knowledge with something valuable to contribute to the company. Remember, you are co-creating the achievement of a vision with them.

Equip your employees to succeed. Make sure employees have everything they need to do their jobs. Remember when you started a new school year and you'd prepare by getting all new school supplies? Why not build just such an opportunity into your department simply by asking each staff member, or the team as a whole, "Do you have everything you need to be as competent as you can be?"

Just as marketplace and customer needs change daily, so do your employees' needs.

Get on the train. Make sure your staff is trained – and retrained – in problem solving and conflict resolution skills. This will help them interact better with you, their teammates, customers and suppliers.

It's common sense: Better communications reduce stress and increase positive outcomes.

Look for success stories ... and tout them. Pay attention to company stories and rituals. Are people laughing at each other or with each other? Do they repeat stories of success or moments of shame? Stay away from participating in discussions that are destructive to people or the organization, and keep success stories alive.

Keep a steady course. If you start an initiative and then drop it, your efforts will backfire, creating employee estrangement. People are exhausted and exasperated from "program du jour" initiatives that engage their passion and then fizzle out when the manager gets bored, fired or moved to another department.

There's a connection between an employee's commitment to an initiative and a manager's commitment to supporting it. A manager's ongoing commitment to keeping people engaged, involved in and excited about the work they do and the challenges they face must be a daily priority.

I've said it once and I'll say it again – your business is going nowhere without your employees. You need them on board and on fire. The best way to do that is to remind them at every turn that they are your business' greatest assets.

If you include them, teach them, and reward them; if you welcome their ideas, ask for feedback and generate enthusiasm, you'll be 99% of the way there.

SHOULD YOU HAVE AN EMPLOYEE HANDBOOK?

As your business grows, your employees will have a lot more questions on what needs to be done, how to do those things, and how their tasks are in line with your company's goals.

One way to give your staff a blueprint of your business and how things should be done is to put together an employee handbook.

Handbooks are fairly easy to compile. Here is a checklist:

- Keep your handbook clear, concise, and compliant with applicable laws.

- Try to anticipate – and answer – every answer your employees might have.

- Start with your company's mission statement at the beginning and briefly explain the purpose of the manual.

- Lay out eligibility for employment, the importance of respecting co-workers and your sexual harassment policies, along with details on the 90-day employment evaluation period.

- Explain compensation, personal safety, placement of government posters and general policies (parking spaces, dress code, smoking).

- Explain your employee benefits plan or plans. Be sure to explain eligibility requirements (exempt and non-exempt employees), health and dental plan premiums, employee retirement plans, stock options, workers' compensation benefits, vacation and holiday schedules and COBRA.

- If you have a company property policy, emphasize that policy. That means making it known that phone systems, Internet, email, and even office supplies are only for business use. If you allow employees some leeway with personal calls or Internet surfing, set clear limitations.

- Lay out your company leave policy, making sure to explain your business' policy for the various types of absence. By law, you must allow employees to serve jury duty with pay. What used to be "maternity leave" is now "family leave," as the number of stay-at-home fathers has grown. Explain how many sick days employees receive, how long they get for bereavement, and what their benefits are for short-term and long-term disability.

- Explain your discipline policy in detail. This is never a comfortable subject, but it's one you can't ignore. Have a documented system in place for conflict resolution and warnings for violating company policy. If these steps don't work out, include sections on at-will employment and grounds for termination.

You can save time and contract the writing and development of your employee handbook out to an employment agency or a business writer. Make sure you design and print a hard copy, along with a file you can place on your Web site for employees to peruse.

PERFORMANCE REVIEWS

Reviews are an opportunity to encourage, motivate and, if necessary, discipline your staff. They are vital to building trust, setting expectations and correcting potential problems.

So how can you do an independent appraisal of your employees performance? Truth is, you probably cannot. On some level, we all have a bias on important issues.

Here are some things to look at when evaluating an employee's performance:

- How would you rate the employee's ability to organize, plan and lead subordinates?

- Does this employee have a warm and sociable attitude toward customers?

- What impression does your employee's personal appearance make?

- How would you rate their ability to get along with others?

- Does this person have the ability to teach and lead others? Are they able to learn and adapt quickly?

- Does this person demonstrate an ability to follow the rules? How well do they look after the equipment or office space they are provided?

- Does this person show up for work, or are they routinely absent without permission?

- How stable is this person? How do they deal with pressure? How confident do they appear? How would you describe their predominant mood?

- How willing is this person to carry out instructions and cooperate with you and fellow employees? Are they a team player? Do you observe passive resistance or blatant argumentative tendencies?

- Is this person able to adapt to changing conditions and learn quickly?

- To what degree does this employee think constructively and take appropriate action? How much supervision does this person require? Are they fair and balanced in decision making?

- How much does this person work conscientiously and in line with instructions? How much do you have to check and verify their work?

- Is there a satisfactory amount of output? Do they over-promise or under-deliver? Are they slow or do they work hard and turn out more work than required?

- To what level do they understand all phases of work? Do they excel at the job or do they lack knowledge in the job or certain areas?

- Is there a consistent level of performance in meeting or exceeding quality standards?

* * *

Ask E-Diva

Dear E-Diva,

I own a bakery and do a great business with customized birthday and wedding cakes. I'm think-ing of opening another store, but don't ask me where. I feel scared. I'm confused about how big I want to grow. My husband says I need to "see the future."

How do you set business goals? I don't even know what to ask myself after asking, "How much money do I want to clear this year?" Help!

Sweeter Icing on the Cake

Dear Sweeter Icing,

Sounds great, but there are some major questions you need to answer before you "see the future" a lot more clearly!

Are you making a profit? Is it enough to handle the overhead in a second location? Can you pay the staff on time? Can you pay your taxes on time? These are just a few questions to start you off.

Also, your question on how much money you want to clear this year should have a very specific answer, especially if it will influence whether or not you expand. How much you clear should be based on information from your current actual sales and your projected sales for the next three years.

Here's something important to remember about expansion: Growing too fast into a new location is a major move. Make sure you study the demographics of the new location and test the market on how your cakes might sell there before you expand.

I think you and your husband have a lot of talking to do about goals and figuring out what will work best for both of you. What you really need is to write a business plan that will help you with financial projections, and that would establish a time table that could help you to know better if you can diversify to other locations.

What is a business plan? Basically, a business plan exactly defines your business, identifies your goals and serves as your company's resume. The basic components in a plan include a current and pro forma balance sheet, an income statement and a cash flow analysis. A good business plan is a crucial part of any loan application.

A good business plan helps you allocate resources properly, (including how you'll repay borrowed money), handle unforeseen complications and make good business decisions.

There's no downside to a business plan because, like a map, it helps you go where you want to go — and not wander around and waste time, money and emotional investments.

E-Diva

* * *

Chapter Seven

Running a Socially Responsible Business

" The first step to leadership is servanthood."
– John C. Maxwell, author, minister and motivational speaker

I've always maintained that to have a successful business, you have to have a sense of community.

By contributing to your community, you're contributing not only to the people who live there, but to your company as well. Communities that are diverse, clean, and productive are the kinds of places that business owners want to embrace. In fact, they're the kinds of places business owners ought to embrace.

The popular term for running such a business is called being "socially responsible," or being a "good corporate citizen."

The definition of being a good corporate citizen varies, from all the reading I've done. I'd say the best definition of being socially responsible is to want your company to be part of the community and the world, while wanting the community and the world to be a part of your company.

* * *

Ask E-Diva

Q: I'm just starting out and I'd love to merge the business side of my business with the community side. How do I get started down that road?

A: Running a socially responsible business is a noble sentiment – but not always easy to do. Start with these building blocks and work your way up from there.

Be environmentally friendly. Recycle mercilessly. Encourage carpooling among staff.

Give people a chance. Hire people with disabilities. Make sure your business is accessible to people in wheelchairs. Be charitably inclined. Find a charity and promote it. Do more than just sponsor events; get involved and encourage your staff to get involved.

Encourage your employees. Encourage your staff to enjoy their life and to maintain a work/life balance. Don't expect them to spend huge amounts of time at their jobs.

Of course, these are just broad brushstrokes that can set you on the path to running a socially responsible company. The real work comes in the details, but if you establish clean business practices, open your hiring doors to everyone, get charitably-minded, and get your employees involved, you're well on the way.

 82

* * *

IT'S GOOD BUSINESS ... AND GOOD FOR THE SOUL

From a business standpoint, running a civic-minded company has a myriad of benefits.

I've found the charitable work we do as a company and the time we spend getting involved in the community not only lets us all sleep better at night, it enables my employees to feel better about their jobs (thus building loyalty and commitment with my staff). It also lets customers know we care about the world outside the four walls of our company.

That gets noticed by the community and the people in it.

Given a choice, consumers would rather do business with a company that cares about the world around it than they would a business that only cares about raking in profits and pleasing shareholders.

I'm not saying you should undertake charitable causes and community outreach programs because it's good for business (although that's definitely the case). For me … well, I just like helping out. If it benefits the business, that's a bonus.

Many companies do very well with a socially responsible mindset.

Take The Body Shop. On its Web site, the shopping mall giant's founder, Dame Anita Roddick, says the company is dedicated to "social responsibility, respect for human rights, the environment and animal protection and an absolute belief in community trade."

The company earned revenues of $602 million in February 2003, $711 million in February 2004, and $803 million in February 2005. For a company that says it just wants to leave the world a better place than it found it, socially responsible business practices sure pay off.

WHAT MAKES A SOCIALLY RESPONSIBLE BUSINESS?

Defining socially responsible business practices means covering a lot of ground. Let's give it a shot. Here are the different aspects, from my experience and research, of such a business.

- **Environmental restoration:** The organization works to protect and restore the environment and promote sustainable development with products, processes, services, and other activities. It is committed to minimizing the use of energy and natural resources and decreasing waste and harmful emissions. The organization integrates these standards into day to day operations.

- **Ethics:** The organization develops and implements ethical standards and practices in dealing with all the organization's stakeholders. The organization's commitment to ethical behavior is widely communicated in an explicit statement and is rigorously upheld.

- **Accountability:** The organization acknowledges that many constituents have legitimate interests in its activities and discloses information in a timely manner so stakeholders can make informed decisions. The stakeholders' need-to-know takes precedence over inconvenience and cost to the organization.

- **Empowerment:** The organization balances the interests of employees, customers, investors, suppliers, affected communities and other stakeholders in strategic objectives as well as day-to-day management and investment decisions. The organization manages its resources conscientiously and effectively, seeking to enhance both financial and human capital.

- **Financial performance and results:** The organization compensates providers of capital with a competitive rate of return while protecting the organization's assets and the sustainability of these returns. The organization's policies and practices are established to enhance long-term growth.

- **Workplace standards:** The organization engages in human resource management practices that promote personal and professional employee development, diversity at all levels and empowerment. The organization regards employees as valued partners in the enterprise, respecting their right to fair labor practices, competitive wages and benefits and a safe, harassment free, family-friendly work environment.

- **Collaborative relationships:** The organization is fair and honest with business partners, including suppliers, distributors, licensees, and agents. The organization promotes and monitors the social responsibility of business partners.

- **Quality products and services:** The organization identifies and responds to the needs and rights of its customers and consumers. It works to provide the highest levels of product and service value, including a strong commitment to integrity, customer satisfaction and safety.

- **Community involvement:** The organization fosters an open relationship with the community in which it operates that is sensitive to the community's culture and needs. The organization plays a proactive, cooperative, and where appropriate, collaborative role in making the community a better place to live and conduct business.

FAST FACT: SOCIAL RESPONSIBILITY IS BIG BUSINESS
Nearly $1 in every $10 of assets under management in the U.S. – an estimated $2.3 trillion out of $24 trillion – is being poured into companies that emphasize some level of social responsibility.

84

THE MARRIAGE OF BUSINESS AND COMMUNITY

By nature, entrepreneurs are idealists.

Certainly the ones I've met are idealistic. Many are college-educated (some, like Bill Gates, non-graduates), and most are driven by political and social issues that influence the way they run their businesses.

Some entrepreneurs, for example, refuse to do business with tobacco companies or with companies that have ties to countries with notorious human rights records, like Haiti or China. Others encourage employees to contribute money to favored political candidates or to actively participate in favorite causes, like Earth Day or AIDS awareness events.

In short, these companies take on the personalities of their founders – for good or for bad. For example, people whose closets are loaded with mink coats may not be too excited about writing a check to People for the Ethical Treatment of Animals.

By disavowing corporate greed and rigidity and crafting politically and culturally active companies in their own images, many business owners are, on the one hand, merely expressing their individuality and rebelliousness, but, as I've said, there's also growing evidence that it can be good for business.

I can't cite you a dollar figure for my own company, but it just feels like we're doing better and are happier and more productive employees when my staff and I engage in community activities – especially those that bring us in direct contact with the disadvantaged and the less fortunate.

Consequently, establishing ethical codes of conduct and acting in a socially conscious manner – both within a company and the community at large – brings tangible rewards above and beyond profits and time invested. Like-minded employees are more productive and will likely stick with a company that shares their particular brand of politics and social awareness.

That's a big bonus in a tight labor market.

According to a Walker Information survey of 1,694 employees, 86% of respondents shared a favorable view of their company's social outreach efforts; 73% said they work in organizations that have written standards of ethical business conduct. Nearly four in 10 worked for organizations that provide ethics-related training, and 31% said their companies had either an ethics officer or ombudsman.

The same sense of loyalty is bred in customers, who are drawn to businesses that share their political and cultural views. In a recent Walker Information poll of consumer trends, 47% of the 1,036 polled said given a level playing field, they would base their final buying decisions on which company was more politically correct. And 70% said they would not – at any price – buy products from a company that was not socially responsible.

In other words, a company earns some points for doing good deeds, but it gets hammered if it indulges in unethical business practices. All things being equal between two otherwise similar businesses, the one that matches a customer's social philosophy will invariably walk away with the business.

It's impossible to quantify just how many entrepreneurs are running their businesses in socially conscious ways, but the fact that more companies are thinking green or supporting other political causes by itself is hardly surprising.

Young business owners in particular are frequently more idealistic and socially conscious (or at least more vocally so) than their established elders. Many younger entrepreneurs aren't married, have no children and have never held a corporate job, a fact that makes them willing and able to risk failure rather than compromise their ideals.

DO THE RIGHT THING

Some resources for the socially conscious business owner:

- **Business for Social Responsibility:** Regards social responsibility and profitability as compatible goals. Offers conferences, educational programs for the public and consulting for members. Call (415) 537-0888 or visit www.bsr.org.
- **Co-Op America:** This national non-profit group helps businesses and individuals solve social and environmental problems. Their website features the Green Pages, a searchable directory of products and services from environmentally and socially conscious businesses. Call (800) 561-GREEN.
- **Social Venture Network:** A 400-member group of business leaders and entrepreneurs, their Web site has information on the group's special initiatives, such as a program to involve businesses in urban areas. Call (415) 561-6501 or visit www.svn.org.

- ***Beyond the Bottom Line: Putting Social Responsibility to Work for Your Business and the World*** **(Touchstone Books) by Joel Makower:** Gives a history of the organization Business for Social Responsibility, as well as advice on making your business socially conscious.
- ***85 Best Business Practices for Socially Responsible Companies*** **(JP Tarcher) by Alan Reder:** Offers practical case studies on how raised social responsibility can increase profitability.
- ***Companies with a Conscience: Intimate Portraits of Twelve Firms That Make a Difference*** **(Citadel Press) by Mary Scott:** Profiles of 12 profitable U.S. companies that demonstrate social responsibility.

A GOODWILL HUNTING CHECKLIST

As most entrepreneurs discover, cultivating socially responsible business practices can make good business sense. It is possible to follow your moral compass and create an ethical business framework.

If beefing up your company's moral fiber seems like a lot of work, consider the alternative. Imagine your up-and-coming, but ethically undisciplined outfit derailed by disgruntled clients, renegade employees, hapless decision-making and a corporate reputation that makes Jerry Springer look like Walter Cronkite. Under these conditions, it's difficult for any company to thrive.

It's not easy for new business owners to juggle the demands of social responsibility with those of a fledgling company. And being "socially responsible" can become quite complicated itself.

According to the Green Journal, an Internet-based, socially responsible business organization, business owners have much to account for when creating politically correct commerce practices: They must consider their company, employees, customers, shareholders, the community, business partners and suppliers, global business and the environment.

Start by looking at resource centers on the Web, like the ones I've listed in this chapter, that have databases of information on corporate citizenship issues and have examples of leadership company practices. When you're doing research, make sure you keep a reasonable monetary and time limit; focus on the ones you can realistically handle. You are already going to have a lot on your hands by opening a new business.

For example, Business for Social Responsibility (BSR) has a package that can help entrepreneurs get going fast. New companies can use the Social Responsibility Starter Kit, which is an introduction to corporate responsibility and identifies ways companies can reflect their own values. You can look in the environment section at energy efficiency and pollution levels. Community involvement is also big. There are lots of creative ways of pitching in without cash donations, like providing the use of your company's facility for a community gathering.

Here's a checklist of questions you should ask yourself about your company – questions

I've asked about my own company's community outreach efforts. They cover a range of issues you should think about as you shape a socially responsible course of action.

It may be impossible (and perhaps isn't even advisable) for any one company to follow through on all of them, all of the time, but by thinking about them, you can get a better feel for how you might approach your corporate relationship with your community and the world at large, and for how you might best contribute to your favorite cause or causes.

- How does your company handle its corporate openness, citizenship and accountability?
- Where does your company advertise (radio, television, print media), and what events do they sponsor?
- Does your company have a corporate code of ethics or principles or a mission statement?
- How does your company react to shareholder resolutions?
- What is your total compensation package? How are your board members compensated? Is your company a member of responsible business organizations?
- Does your company manufacture alcohol, tobacco or weapons?

The way companies treat their employees is also important. The following questions address management's role in creating a diverse, ethical workplace:

- Does your company have women and minorities in senior management and on the board of directors?

87

- Does your company have responsible workplace policies and practices including nondiscriminatory employment and positive labor relations?
- Does your company have comprehensive healthcare and benefits packages for employees, domestic partners and their families?
- Does your company have on-site daycare, an employer-supported childcare center or elder care?
- Does your company offer profit-sharing or gain-sharing programs, a stock purchasing plan or an employee stock option program?
- Does your company have flexible scheduling, flex-time, telecommuting and job-sharing available?
- Does your company offer continuing education and training programs for employees?
- Does your company have a socially and environmentally responsible 401(k) investment plan?

Most of my company's socially responsible efforts are community based. In other words, they're local. That's the best fit for us. That said, global consciousness is a big buzzword in the early 21st century. Here are some questions to ask yourself as you ponder how your business should relate to the world around it:

- Do your responsibilities extend beyond your immediate community, town or city?
- Does your company have a global code of conduct on working conditions and labor

sourcing as well as human rights?

- Does your company have business activities in countries known for their oppressive governments or human rights abuses (such as Burma, Nigeria or China)?
- Does your company have effective policies and practices addressing child labor, wages, worker health and safety?

Vendors, suppliers and other business partners must be factored in as well. If one of the things you're selling is your company's social responsibility, you need to do business with other companies that also uphold those standards.

It's an imperfect world, so while it might do no harm to be linked with a company that serves veal cutlets at its company picnic, you probably want to avoid a supplier who gets all their goods from sweatshops in Southeast Asia. Such connections only undermine your credibility as a socially responsible corporate citizen. Here are some questions to ask:

- Does your company have a code of conduct, standards and guidelines for all their suppliers, vendors and subcontractors worldwide?
- Does your company, its vendors or subcontractors use child, forced or prison labor?
- Does your company have supplier standards for products, materials and workers?
- Is your company purchasing socially and environmentally responsible products?
- Is your company using women-owned, minority and responsible vendors?

DON'T GO OVERBOARD

Creating a socially conscious company is a noble heartfelt goal for any entrepreneur, young or old. It's a good business practice, and its' the right thing to do.

However, don't become so relentless about promoting causes and policing your vendors that you drive business away or get caught not practicing everything you preach.

Give some thought to how much of a good-faith effort you want to make to go green and be socially responsible, because customers will hold you to the standard you set for yourself. Fall from that standard, sometimes even just a little bit, and they will not hesitate to criticize you and take their business elsewhere. Decide what you can reasonably accomplish and don't overreach because it can backfire.

Also, most employees have limits on how many lectures they can sit through from management on the impact of discarded pencil shavings on global deforestation or the importance of wearing cosmetics that weren't tested on animals to the big sales pitch in Chicago.

Getting socially like-minded staffers on board is great, but don't force everyone to think the same. Set standards and practices that are important to you, but don't make them so rigid or difficult to achieve that you wind up creating internal conflict. Even the most socially responsible companies must make compromises and operate within the limits of the society around them.

Just ask Ben & Jerry's, the ice cream company that is perhaps one of the most high-profile and successful companies to make its name by touting its ethical business practices and its corporate donor program.

A few years ago they decided to give away gallons of extra diluted ice cream to local pig farmers instead of washing it down the drain, as most ice cream companies do. Here was a seemingly feel-good corporate story: Ben & Jerry's solves a minor environmental problem while local pigs get to chow down on Rain Forest Crunch, Cherry Garcia and other tasty ice cream delights.

Or so everyone thought.

Unfortunately, their act of benevolence turned unexpectedly ugly and fatal. Piglets that happily slurped Ben & Jerry's homemade sugar water never made it to 600-pound adulthood. They suddenly began expiring at 200 pounds, victims of oddly humanlike arteriosclerosis. And according to local pig farmers, the slaughtered pigs yielded a fattier pork.

Unfortunately, neither Ben & Jerry's nor the farmers had explored the implications of feeding pigs premium ice cream, and the experiment was quickly dropped.

As you can see from the setbacks suffered by Ben & Jerry's, idealism isn't always easily translated into a marketing or business strategy. Once you've decided to make your new business a socially responsible one, you've got to walk the walk. Make sure you understand the cultural terrain you're about to navigate.

One last point: It's all well and good to toot your own horn, to clear your throat and point to yourself at cocktail parties (or in glossy advertisements) when the talk turns to socially responsible businesses. But don't get too caught up in yourself. If your green image is seen as nothing more than a marketing ploy, it won't work with customers.

Corporate responsibility may be newly fashionable, but its not new: Corporations have been engaged in socially conscious activity for years as a way to burnish their image and to return some good to the society that nourishes them.

That said, there's no reason why you can't merge your social views with your business views as your venture grows. If anything, knowing your business is making a difference culturally as well as commercially is quite an achievement for a young entrepreneur.

Definitely something to tell your grandchildren about.

SO WHAT ARE YOU WAITING FOR?

There's no end of good causes that can use a helping hand. Here are just a few ideas.

- Providing food for the elderly or homeless. Help financially or by serving meals.
- Audio books for the blind: Audiotape producers are always looking for readers and funding.
- Hold an American Red Cross blood drive at your place of business.
- Help with fund-raising for any number of good social causes.

- Let a spokesperson for Big Brothers/Big Sisters speak at your workplace.
- If you're in the food business, donate excess food to homeless shelters.
- If you're in the music business, arrange for small, free concerts at homes for the elderly.
- If you're a financial person, offer to give some counseling at a neighborhood center on budgeting or debt management.
- Promote adopt-a-pet programs at your local humane society.
- Have employees contribute old clothing to give to the needy.
- Work with a local environmental group to clean up a neglected natural area.
- Print up some t-shirts and do some construction work for Habitat for Humanity
- Consider sports sponsorships, especially for teams from disadvantaged neighborhoods.
- Promote literacy programs in connection with schools or community organizations.
- Young people these days need mentors; adults who can teach them about life. Look into existing mentoring programs.
- Talk to your local social services people. They can steer your to hundred of additional worthwhile opportunities.

Limit your involvement to a few ventures. It's far better to work with two or three causes where you can make a real difference than to spread yourself so thin that your money and efforts have little impact.

 90

MORE RESOURCES

There are many resources for those who want to run a socially-responsible *and* profitable business. Here are just a few:

- Net Impact "is a network of more than 12,000 new-generation leaders committed to using the power of business to improve the world."
- Worthwhile Magazine promotes "Work with purpose, passion and profit." Their editorial mission is "to put purpose and passion on the same plane as profit. Worthwhile offers a roadmap for business success that is more personally fulfilling and socially responsible."
- Business for Social Responsibility is a nonprofit "global organization that helps member companies achieve success in ways that respect ethical values, people, communities and the environment. BSR provides information, tools, training and advisory services to make corporate social responsibility an integral part of business operations and strategies".
- Business Ethics is "the magazine for corporate responsibility." Their Web site has a wonderful list of resources for those interested in "progressive business and investing."

E-Diva
Dr. Rae Pearson

Chapter Eight
Marketing Your Way to Millions

"I had to make my own living and my own opportunity! But I made it! Don't sit down and wait for the opportunities to come. Get up and make them!"

-- Madam C.J. Walker, America's first black female millionaire

I always say your company's success depends upon your ability to run it.

Sure, you can surround yourself with good people, but in the end you have to be calling the shots. Only you can make the decisions that ensure success.

I know you're probably thinking, "How do entrepreneurs take a great idea and then fund it, produce it, market it and distribute it so successfully?"

Here's the short answer to that question (the rest of this chapter is the long version). You walk with your idea every step of the way, making sure your company is run the way *you* want it to be run. This means hiring the right people, making the right decisions and taking some risks.

That's the only way to get ahead.

None of this is going to come easy, but there are some proven methods for getting off to a good start. First you write a business plan, then work like crazy for funding, dive in to find some office space, hire a staff, develop and implement a marketing plan, and, finally, hustle your products to shipping docks and store shelves on time and under budget.

Sure, that seems like a large load carry. But I did it and I know you can, too.

MARKETING YOUR WAY TO MILLIONS

Harvey Mackay, author of the best-selling business book *Swim with the Sharks without Being Eaten Alive*, said marketing is creating a condition that allows the buyer to convince him or herself to buy.

From my experience, I'd have to agree. But you have to crack the code and figure out what that "condition" is.

91

I have a girlfriend who used to joke with our friends that someday she'd become a big-time entrepreneur. Even in high school she'd make jewelry and macramé items and sell them. Everyone used to get a big kick out of it, but she knew what she was doing.

Fresh from a few freelance advertising assignments for local ad agencies, she got the nerve to open her own shop (a creative services and marketing company that does a lot of promotional work using graphics and visual media). Partnering with another friend who could handle more of the business end, the two had an admirable group of clients in a few short years.

What really shone about this duo was their marketing prowess. After creating a business plan, they put a system into place to achieve the growth they desired. Though light on monetary figures, this plan was a blueprint for all the firm's marketing efforts and growth. With client profiles as well as promotional strategies and tactics, it cataloged promotions that were successes (and failures) and projected future needs (like training and new equipment).

This marketing plan serves the girls, keeping them focused on their core business values. It keeps a balance (especially after they expanded operations onto the Web) rather than allowing one segment or one client to become an overwhelming portion of their business.

With both women making hundreds of cold calls and setting up a shoestring advertising campaign, aggressive promotion was also in their marketing plan. The hardest part, my friend said, was managing these and the print ad responses they would get.

Every year the partners review the plan (and actually look forward to doing so). They first get together in an informal, relaxed setting (no phones ringing, no clients demanding immediate attention) to discuss the effectiveness of the plan and brainstorm ideas for the coming year.

Then (usually in a more structured session a few days later) they rewrite the plan, fitting their analyses and new ideas into the existing document.

They estimate their business grew 100% (that is not a typo) the first year after institution of the marketing plan. Business has continued to grow at an astounding rate of 50% or more annually since then. The firm now has five employees and a pool of freelance talent.

These girls warn new marketers not to get caught up in making your plans too formal, but rather to make sure the format is easy to use. You have to remember, the most successful plans are those that don't try to be anyone else's. Think back to all those previous jobs you held (especially the bad ones) and how they practiced business. These guidelines from your past will show you how not to run your business.

MARKETING MATCHMAKING

Before you begin writing your marketing plan, think about how you want to market your business. Most products and services depend on good marketing for their ultimate success.

For instance, lighting fixtures are a necessity and, in a way, sell themselves.

But why should someone buy yours? That is the crucial step in marketing – getting inside the head of consumers and figuring out what they want; what attracts them. How do you make your product or service seem not just useful and attractive but necessary and vital?

Marketing your business isn't unlike pursuing a romantic interest and going out on a date. You want to be attractive; you want to embody all the qualities the other person desires. You'll put on flattering clothes and make jokes to display affection. Does the other person like movies? What do you know, so do you! Does he or she like climbing mountains, crossword puzzles, sleeping late or jazz music? How fast can you get to Tower Records and buy some John Coltrane?

It's an old refrain, but it's still true: Don't sell what you've got, sell what they want. Like a young romantic, learn all you can about your lover's likes, dislikes and expectations, and then do everything you can to embody what he or she most desires.

What does this mean in practice? First, identify the types of people you think will (or already do) make up your customer base; categorize them by age, sex, income and educational level and residence. To start out, target only those customers who are most likely to purchase your product or service.

In other words, if you're selling surfboards, stay out of Minneapolis.

As your customer base expands, you can consider modifying your marketing plan to include other types of customers.

Here's a quick marketing exercise. Your marketing plan should answer these questions (and don't peek at the answers because there aren't any):

- Who are your customers? Define your target market(s).

- Are your markets growing? Steady? Declining?

- Are your markets large enough to expand?

- How will you attract, hold and increase your market share?

- What pricing strategy have you devised?

THE PRICE IS RIGHT: PRICING AND SALES

The price you charge for your product or service is actually a marketing strategy.

While you need to determine a base price to cover your expenses, the final price is more the result of customer perception and where you want to place yourself in the market relative to other companies. Get a feel for the pricing strategy of competitors in your market area and for the averages in your industry nationwide. Then figure out how you want to be competitive: Should you sell slightly under price and pull customers with the idea that your product offers savings? Or should you slightly overprice, attracting customers with the claim that you offer higher quality?

GET YER YA-YAS OUT: ADVERTISING AND PUBLIC RELATIONS

Much of your marketing plan comes down to advertising and promotion. How will you get the word out about your fabulous goods and services?

Many business owners operate under the mistaken concept that a good business promotes itself, so they channel money that should be used for advertising and promotions to other areas of the business. This is a mistake. Advertising and promotions are the lifeline of a business and should be treated as such. Without them, most people won't know you have a business at all.

For small and emerging businesses, most advertising is of the shoestring variety. A limited budget, however, doesn't mean you have to sacrifice a good promotional campaign.

Instead of plowing $10,000 into a television ad campaign, spend half of that on a good public relations campaign that can get your company's name into industry trade publications. Many entrepreneurs offer their services as speakers at industry and business functions and appear on radio and TV talk shows as "industry experts." Tie your company to a well-known industry Web site and join your local chamber of commerce. All these ideas are either low-cost or no-cost and provide you with the opportunity to get your company's name out there.

If and when you do create a traditional ad campaign, remember one thing: Stay focused. Develop short, descriptive copy that clearly identifies your goods or services and your location and price. Use catchy phrases to arouse the interest of your readers, listeners or viewers. Remember, the more care and attention you devote to your marketing program, the more successful your business will be.

Finally, don't confuse advertising with public relations; they are distinctly different. With advertising, space or time in the mass media must be paid for. With public relations, coverage in the mass media, if any, is not paid for. With advertising, the content of your message and when it appears is determined by you. In public relations, interpretation of the message and the timing is in the hands of the media.

Got it?

ANATOMY OF A MARKETING PLAN

Getting the product to the user and all the decisions made to facilitate this movement is called marketing. Simply put, marketing activities and strategies result in making products available that satisfy customers, while making profits for the companies that offer those products.

Marketing is an all-encompassing activity in which the aim is to focus the various efforts of producing, pricing, promoting and placing the product in people's hands – that is, those selected groups called target markets. A good marketing plan is comprised of a cornucopia of business outreach ideas, ranging from advertising to sales to public relations. A focus on what the customer wants is essential to successful marketing campaigns.

This customer orientation must also be balanced with the company's objective of maintaining a profitable enough sales volume for the company to continue to do business. There really is no time frame for completing and executing a marketing plan; marketing is a creative, ever-changing orchestration of all the activities needed to promote your business.

WHO ARE YOU?

Before you map out where you want your marketing plan to take you, analyze where you are now. If you've already started your business, how have you positioned it in the market? Is this how your customers see you?

Ask some of them for feedback – either informally, approaching a few that you trust, or use a form customers can fill out themselves that summarizes your business, including its philosophy and its strengths and weaknesses. Be as objective as possible.

WHO ARE YOUR CUSTOMERS?

To market successfully, you need to define who you're selling to. If you say "everyone," you need to rethink your answer. Even the largest companies don't market blindly to every individual. They break their audiences down into distinct profiles, or niche markets, and create messages and vehicles designed to reach each segment.

Define your niche markets as clearly and specifically as possible. If you're reaching out to businesses, describe which type, including the industry, revenue level, location and other important characteristics. If you're targeting particular types of consumers, define them using both demographics (physical characteristics) and psychographics (psychological characteristics).

95

Demographics outline such factors as age, sex, marital status, geographic location, education and income levels. Psychographics offer insight into trends, buying habits, market segments and so on. If you identify several market segments, rank them in order of priority.

Even if you've done this before, you may need to do some research to get all the information you need. There are a variety of resources, many of them free. For instance, *American Demographics* magazine has a Web site (**www.demographics.com**) that offers access to articles about various consumer and business market segments.

Trade associations and publications are often great places to start your research, especially if you're reaching out to businesses. Many trade associations have Web sites, and many publications are also available on the Internet. For information about consumer audiences in your region, try your state or county's department of economic development.

In addition, the SBA offers limited help with market research. Find out more about its services at **www.sba.gov.**

The exact kind of information you'll need will depend on the type of consumer you're targeting. For instance, if you're selling a product to homeowners in Anytown, USA find out what percentage of people own homes in Anytown. What is the average household income? Do most homeowners have children? Where do homeowners shop? The more specific your profiles are the more valuable they will be.

* * *

Ask E-Diva

Dear E-Diva,

I keep hearing people talk about branding. What is branding? I have a new company and wonder if branding is for me. Please share your thoughts.

Mr. Looking for a Bigger Market Curiosity,

 96

Dear Mr. Curiosity,

When I started my business, all we talked about was marketing our services, rather than making ourselves a brand. But branding in the last 20 years has become a dominant concept in marketing, and a science within itself.

So to your question: What is branding? I read a book on the subject that said, "Over time, a blend of image, identity and reputation combine to create simple, clear perceptions." In a very real way, that's what branding is all about. It's the personal connection you create about your product or service to reach your targeted customer market. It's how you distinguish yourself from your competition and how you capture your part of the market share.

In making all this happen, you must make sure your marketing materials have a recognizable identity, with a consistent logo, motto or tag line. For example, when you see the Buick commercials featuring Tiger Woods, you associate the Buick emblem and Tiger, a master in his sport. You have a respected, more than credible recognized sports personality saying he chooses this car with a known car maker, suggesting that he thinks Buick creates "masters," too.

Tiger, indeed.

Here are some tips:

- *Get the public relations pros to open markets for you. A good PR agency can give you great ideas to get you started.*

- *Sign up for media coaching (so you learn to speak in public with ease) and find speechwriters to help you say what you want to say most effectively. Or, go with a design team to develop newsworthy presentations about your product or business that give you some media coverage.*

- *Get notable endorsements that knock the socks off your customer base. Don't let one (or ten!) turn downs stop you.*

- *Create a memorable way to demonstrate your product or service.*

Brand building requires emotional impact, repetition, and time to become known in the market. Your goal is product association with your company name. For instance, when someone says "soda pop," people immediately think of the brands Coca-Cola or Pepsi. Remember, a lot of response to your product is based on media exposure, repetitive logo identification and the passion the general public has for buying it.

I would suggest you start off slowly, and over time keep adding to your media and public relations plan. As I mentioned before, if this area is not within your expertise, hire a professional.

E-Diva

97

* * *

THE COMPETITION ANGLE

Keeping an eye on your competitors is not just important from a marketing aspect, it's simply good business. It's good to know who your closest competitors are, and even who your indirect competitors are. Are their businesses coming or faltering? What does their advertising look like? What about their brochures and Web sites?

In your marketing plan, include a section where you describe the strengths and weaknesses of your competitors and how their products differ from yours.

In addition to writing a brief profile of your competition in your marketing plan, keep an ongoing file on each of your competitors. Keep track of their advertising and promotional materials and their pricing strategies. Review these files periodically, determining when and how often they advertise, sponsor promotions and offer sales. Study their ads, promotion copy and what sales strategies they're using.

For example, is their copy short? Do they use testimonials? How much do they reduce prices for sales? Studying the competition keeps you abreast of the game, and sometimes it helps keep you from making the same mistakes others have made.

SETTING YOUR SIGHTS

Now that you have a sense of where you are, you can decide where you want to go. What will you try to accomplish with your marketing plan? Do you want to announce your presence to your target audience? Increase sales in certain markets? Change the perception of your business? Generate more store traffic? Enter a new market in which you may not have much experience?

Outline each of your goals separately, and be specific. While you should be optimistic about what you can accomplish, be realistic and keep expectations limited. Setting a goal to increase sales by 80% may be self-defeating since achieving that level of new sales usually takes special circumstances – such as an outstanding new product or a significant competitor's demise.

Remember, you need to support each goal with concrete action, and actions take time and money. If you set multiple goals for yourself, be sure to prioritize them so you can spread out your resources in the best possible way.

PLAN OF ACTION

This is the heart of your game plan. For each goal you've outlined, create a strategy, complete with your key message (kind of like a smaller mission statement) and the steps that will help you accomplish the goal.

Brainstorm about the best ways to reach each of your goals. What are the most cost-effective but efficient vehicles for getting your message out? You have many forms of advertising to choose from: Newspapers, radio, television, magazines, outdoor billboards and so on.

There are also direct marketing items like postcards, sales letters, fliers, business reply cards, newsletters or toll-free response numbers. You could go for a softer sell using public relations efforts such as publicity, special events, public speaking engagements, sponsorships and opinion polls.

Perhaps you can accomplish your objectives and cut costs by teaming up with related, non-competing businesses for in-store promotions or cross-promotional campaigns. On-line promotional opportunities are more abundant than ever, so consider designing a company Web site or uploading your product's information into a newsgroup or special interest forum.

PUTTING IT IN WRITING

Here's a sample of how to write a goal outlining your strategy, key message and tactics.

Strategy: Position myself as the market leader in home inspections in my community.

Key message: The Home Inspectors is a reputable, trustworthy name in home inspections.

TACTICS:

- Approach local community colleges about teaching a home-buying class.
- Propose a feature story to a local paper about "10 Things to Look for When Buying a Home," with you as the expert to be quoted.
- Create a brochure titled "Secrets of Buying a Home." Offer it free to people who call.
- Issue a press release about the free brochure to local media.
- Send informational brochures to real estate agents and mortgage brokers who refer home buyers to home inspectors.

For each step you plan, keep asking yourself "Why should I do this?"

In other words, make sure your tactics match your goals and resources. Don't do a widespread mailing to reach a small segment of customers. Don't do big, splashy promotions if you really can't afford them. Smaller, more frequent communications are much more effective if your budget is limited.

For example, a small accounting firm wanted to increase its exposure in local newspapers. The owner made a $10,000 donation to a local charity's annual gala, believing this would make a great news story. While the gesture was greatly appreciated by the charity and its supporters, that money represented the majority of the firm's annual marketing budget.

In return, the owner got one brief story in the local paper. If the organization's goal was to become more philanthropic, the donation was an effective gesture. However, the original goal was to increase publicity, so the money would have been better spent on a diverse program with more components.

Finally, be sure the promotions you've selected project the right image. If your audience is small-town and conservative, urban angst and anorexic models won't sell your appliances. Similarly, if your customers are hip and sophisticated, make sure to project a cutting-edge imagine with sharp visuals and design.

MARKETING BUDGET BASICS: MONEY + TIME = BUSINESS

One of the most tragic myths in business is you can skimp on, or entirely do without, a marketing budget. Marketing costs money, sometimes lots of it, but it is not an optional expense. It's a priority, especially in times of slow cash flow. After all, how are you going to attract more business during the slow times if you don't tell customers about your business?

Take a realistic look at how much money you have to spend on marketing. While you shouldn't overextend yourself, it's critical that you allot adequate funds to reach your markets. If you find you don't have the budget to tackle all your markets, pick the most important and go after them one by one.

For each of your tactics, break down its estimated cost. For example, a brochure includes writing, photography, graphic design, film, printing, and delivery – not to mention, in some cases, mailing.

To save money, get creative. Maybe you can barter with a printer or write the copy yourself. Just be careful that such strategies don't backfire. If you're selling Jaguars, a cheap-looking ad or brochure will kill you. If you can't afford everything, adjust your plan and accomplish some of the most important tactics well.

Finally, decide how much time each tactic will take and set deadlines. Some tactics will require multiple steps, and those should be outlined.

Get out a calendar and plot all the marketing tasks you've just set for yourself. Can you do it? Can you delegate or hire someone to help you? Again, be realistic about what you can accomplish and trim your goals if you think you're taking on too much. It's better to start with smaller, more achievable goals than to burn yourself out with an overly ambitious program that you'll end up discarding a few months later.

DON'T STOP NOW

You now have a well-researched, realistic, detailed marketing plan that will guide your business through the dangerous battlefield of modern commerce. On the way, you've gained knowledge and expertise about your market that will prove invaluable as you adjust and revise your strategy in the months and years ahead.

100

Here's one thing I've learned over the years: Don't put your marketing plan on a shelf and forget about it. It should be a living document that grows and changes over time. Review it periodically, at least twice a year. As your business grows, you must evaluate the success of your initial strategies, shifting or increasing the scope of your marketing to adjust to changing market factors or new business horizons. If you find something is not working, change it.

Consistency and continuity delivered with a dash of creativity give you the formula for successful marketing.

KEEP ON TRUCKIN'

At last, the planning is over, the funding is in place, and your product or service is ready to go.

Now how do you get it to your customers?

If you offer a service, you either have an office where customers come (like an accounting firm) or you go to them (such as a house cleaning business). If you are opening a retail store, then all you do is open your doors (and pray).

If you're selling by catalog or through the Internet, your products will be flying through the mail to their destination. However, if you're hoping to see your revolutionary product shining on the shelves of Wal-Mart, Bloomingdale's or in local supermarkets throughout your country, you have another hurdle before you make your first sale: Distribution.

Distribution means getting your product to retailers and convincing them to buy it and carry it in their stores. Generating initial sales is no picnic for young entrepreneurs, who are new, unproven business owners selling new, unproven products with no track record of business success. When retailers look at an entrepreneur's product, they don't just worry about whether the product will sell; they worry whether the entrepreneur's business will be around in two months.

Entrepreneurs must work extremely hard – and be extremely creative – to generate their first sales to retailers. Most of the time all you can do is cart your samples from store to store hoping for a bite. But you can also try to get picked up by a distributor or a distribution network.

These are companies that represent a variety of products (made by a range of manufacturers) they try to sell to retailers; distributors also handle all the paperwork, physically move the merchandise and take a cut of the profits.

For manufacturers who prefer not to sell their products themselves or who want to get into stores that only work with distributors, a distribution network provides an invaluable service.

However, getting a distributor to carry your product is usually much harder than selling directly to retailers or to consumers, who only compare your product to competing products. The distribution network, which can only represent a limited number of items, also compares your product to all the other non-competing products it could potentially sell.

A distributor's goal is simple: To earn the most money for the least effort.

I know a man in Wisconsin who got a fast start selling his product, a specialized showerhead, thanks to the television home shopping network QVC. When the network aired a segment showcasing products from Wisconsin inventors, his product was chose as "Best of the Show."

Do you think that initial success helped him get placed with a distributor? Unfortunately, it didn't. He learned large retailers and distributors often won't talk to any new business until it's been around for a few years.

While my friend advises young entrepreneurs to try QVC, you must understand its not easy getting onto the channel. They see thousands and thousands of products each day, and they can pick just a few. It was only because of his participation in a trade show sponsored by QVC that his product was picked up.

Once my friend's showerhead was tapped by QVC, he knew his product would create a buzz. He told me it sold out even before he got on air! What happened was the hosts sold his product before he had a chance to pitch it. They sold 2, 800 units in a matter of minutes.

The product was ideal for television because it offered a powerful demonstration – QVC could cue a short video on the product and play it heavily in its product demo rotation. When QVC wound up overselling the product, my friend had to scramble to replace inventory.

Because QVC was so happy with the product they offered my friend a juicy three-year exclusivity contract. This would have made him a wealthy man, but he turned it down.

He said no, but did give them a year of exclusivity for a nice chunk of money.

Despite being a hit on QVC, my friend's product wasn't ready for the big name distributors. The strength of his product was in his demonstration, and major retailers want products that sell based on a package.

So he concentrated on catalogs like Miles Kimball and Damark instead. Today, his showerhead is in more than 35 catalogs, and he estimates last year's sales at more than $1 million.

That was the ticket. Catalog success got his product picked up by a few distributors and placed into retailers such as Kmart and Menards. He also has placement scattered throughout hardware stores nationwide, where the showerhead is selling well. Once my friend had established his sales potential and generated some momentum, he finally got the widespread distribution he was looking for.

Why won't distributors give a new product a chance? Well, setting up sales training and paperwork for a new product is a ton of work, and who wants to spend the time (and money) unless they're sure the product will sell? There isn't a magic formula for getting your product into major retailers, it just takes hard work.

102

My friend teaches us some important lessons. By having an introductory stage where he sold to a limited market, he was able to give extra attention (and promotional efforts) to that market. To entice distributors to pick up his product and sell it to their retail customers, he promised distributors special promotions, demonstrations, extra-long payment terms, frequent restocking services and any other services he thought they might want.

Another reason to limit your market initially: You probably can't afford to launch a product in more than one market.

My friend used every tactic to help his business succeed. After his first sales, he used that momentum to line up a larger network. Remember even if you get a distributor to carry your product, don't think your work is done (always keep marketing and promoting!). You must do everything possible on your own to make sure the distributor's agents are successful and that your product keeps selling once placed. Retailers will drop a product if it doesn't produce sales, and distributors will drop you if retailers start dropping your product.

Consider hiring a demo company (a service that places people in stores to offer customers free samples). While they aren't as motivated or successful demonstrating your product as you would be, they'll make a few sales for you. Also try running newspaper ads, radio promotions, in-store seminars and sponsoring area events.

Don't worry about making money at first (remember what I keep telling you – patience pays off). Worry instead about creating sales momentum. Profits will come once you have a wide distribution network. To reach that goal, you need the biggest promotional budget you can afford and an intense personal sales effort when you start out. As my friend realized, entrepreneurs can't rely on the product (or its packaging) to make sales.

You've got to hustle to get your product off the ground. If you hustle – and believe in yourself – word will get out about you and your company.

* * *

Ask E-Diva

Dear E-Diva,

My husband and I have been in business for five years. How do we gain visibility in the community? We advertise, we work in our church community, but I think we are missing something. How do we gain visibility?

Mr. and Mrs. Low Profile

Dear Mr. and Mrs. Low Profile,

I think all business people think corporate advertising will do the trick. I found there are seven areas that work to get more exposure. When gaining visibility the following has worked for me:

1. ***Developing a Positive Mental Attitude.*** *People love to be around people with a consistent, persistent attitude of cheerfulness and optimism is always notice.*

2. ***Setting Priorities.*** *The ability to establish relevant job tasking from the irrelevant job tasking when assigned.*

3. ***Paying attention to your overall image.*** *The way you look and communicate on the outside is a direct reflection of your company. It's a good idea to dress for a position and act like you have authority.*

4. ***Developing Competence.*** *You must be perceived a being good at what you do.*

5. ***Always upgrade your work related skills.*** *Continually look to educate.*

6. ***Join well-known charitable organizations.*** *Be by donating your services.*

7. ***Join professional associations.*** *Look for those related to your business.*

Oh! Here are a few other ways to gain visibility … WRITE A BOOK, Get a TV show or Radio Show…

E-Diva

* * *

Chapter Nine

Figuring Out an Exit Strategy

" We are the miraculous, the true wonders of this world. Free to choose our ends, and our new beginnings."

– Maya Angelou, from her poem "A Brave and Startling Truth"

I'm not too keen on retirement – not with all the fun I'm having running my company.

The problem with being retired is that you never know what day it is, what time it is, where you are supposed to be, or what you're supposed to be doing.

As a friend of mine said, it's a lot like working for the government.

But the day will come when you will want to sell your company and blaze new trails elsewhere. Hopefully, that day will come on your terms.

Some folks sell because they have to. Lousy market conditions, bad business decisions or simple burnout often cause business owners to hang the "for sale" sign on their front door.

While everyone's circumstances are different, there are the two main catalysts that spur business owners to sell their businesses: The need for cash and the need to move on; to take on another career or lifetime challenge.

No matter how you reach the decision, selling your business is a difficult step, and this chapter will guide you through it. Be clear about your motivations and make sure it's the right thing to do.

Most reasons to sell fall under one or more of the following categories:

- **Emotional:** This is the most common reason. Owners are bored or burned out, while some have other interests and would rather spend their time, energy and money pursuing them. Others simply don't want the stress of running a business anymore.

- **Lifestyle changes:** Many business owners grow tired of the long hours running a business requires; some, want to spend time with or start a family; others have new business ideas they'd like to try, and some may have health concerns that force them to slow down. Still others may decide it's time to retire – they may be 35 or 65.

- **Personal economics:** Often business owners want to liquidate or diversify money that is tied up in the business. They may still want to participate in the business under a management contract with a new owner.

- **Business economics:** A growing company requires the business owners to put a significant amount of the profits back into the company to support increased inventory and receivables. When this is not desirable, it may be an opportune time to sell.

Whether circumstances force them to sell or they merely want out, many business owners find they just can't bear selling their own businesses, and if they do, they wind up jumping into another entrepreneurial effort, unable to shake the desire for the adrenaline rush of owning their own company.

Others may decide to sell but then stay on as part of the business – while they are relieved of the burden of daily decision making, they can still make big money as a high-ranking consultant, board member or even vice president.

Then there are those entrepreneurs who never consider selling at all, and who instead wind up expanding their businesses through a merger or acquisition. To end the chapter, we'll look at the other side of the equation: How to buy companies.

RED FLAGS: IS IT TIME TO GET OUT?

For centuries, gypsies, seers and other spiritualists have made a good living gazing into crystal balls and telling people whether a piano is going to fall on their heads or if true love is lurking around the corner (sometimes both on the same day, and with the same result). Debate continues to rage over the accuracy of such predictions, but even the Titanic had a fortune teller on board.

A grizzled business owner doesn't have to read tea leaves to see into the future. There are a few danger signs you can learn to recognize that can help tell you if agony, catastrophe or the end of your business are on the horizon. If your company exhibits three or more of the following signs, you may want to consider whether it's time to jump ship and sell your business:

- **Your company is experiencing repeated losses.** Recurring losses are bad enough, but when you're financing your losses with additional debt, the problem becomes even more critical. Develop financial goals, sound forecasts, a strategy to achieve the goals and a short-term plan to meet your immediate cash flow requirements.

- **Your industry is experiencing a downturn or an explosion in growth.** Neither of these alone is cause for panic, but each should trigger an aggressive response from your company. Do you know what's going on in the market? Are you responding to industry trends? Your company must be equally prepared to handle a downturn, upswing or new product rollout by the competition.

- **Your company is experiencing capacity issues and high overhead.** Analyze your overhead costs, including administrative, labor and fixed costs such as buildings and vehicles to determine where you can modify spending. If your company has excess capacity in three of five locations, challenge your managers to balance the work flow better.

- **Access to a key product line or supplier is evaporating.** If such a loss is on the horizon for your company, you'd better be evaluating alternative suppliers or products and addressing the short-term impact of the loss on your company. While an aggressive response may be warranted, careful consideration should also be given to slowing overhead and distribution costs.

- **Your company is branching out into new and unrelated business lines.** Expanding your product line can be good, but be cautious of forays into areas totally unrelated to your core product or service. You may not have the expertise to sustain the new push. More importantly, make sure you've properly planned the expansion.

- **Your company manages for income and not cash flow.** Some companies fail to ensure they have enough in their checking accounts to meet their monthly obligations, focusing instead on short-term income – a sure-fire recipe for failure. While quarterly income is a valued benchmark by Wall Street's standards, don't overemphasize it at the expense of cash flow.

- **Your company is experiencing very rapid growth.** Paradoxically, companies can grow themselves into trouble. The cash flow from increased sales may be insufficient to meet your working capital requirements needed to support those sales. Consider borrowing against receivables and inventory and allowing the quality of those assets to support your growth.

- **Your company has failed to differentiate its product.** Whether you provide a product or a service, you must differentiate it from your competition. There are only three ways to do that – by service, quality or price – and even then, you must be smart about how you market your differentiation.

- **Your company is overly reliant on one product or one customer.** You may be successful now, but what will happen at the next economic downturn? Invest in research, development and marketing so you're ready to augment your core product and attract new customers.

- **Your board of directors (or advisors) is not actively involved in the management of your company.** A good board will probe, ask tough questions, stay informed, expect reasonable responses to their questions, demand access to your senior management and stay abreast of industry trends – in short, it will push you to be a better leader. If your board isn't doing that, recruit a new one.

A NEW COAT OF PAINT DOESN'T HURT

If you are looking to sell, freshen up the business a little to make it more attractive. Here are some tips from top brokers on how to approach the potential sales of your business:

- Refocus your perspective from saving taxes to building profits. While it's a generally accepted practice to allocate revenues to a wide range of fringe benefits to lower taxes, the aim of reduced profitability doesn't help when a sale is contemplated.

- Rethink the way the assets on the balance sheet look. Sell off unproductive real estate. That way, you'll realize additional cash even before the sale of the business.

- Mentor a replacement who can assume command if you or a new owner is disabled or absent.

THE SALES PITCH

So how do you do it? How do you cash out your business for a price that would make the Sultan of Dubai strap on a drool bucket? Many important factors that come into play when you plan to sell your business.

There are so many ways to sell a business. Generally, the idea behind selling your business is to tout it, locate the most qualified buyer and obtain the best price and terms to complete a transaction.

Sounds simple, right?

Ha. The process is arduous, time-consuming and frustrating. In one case I've seen from a marketing company I knew, the process was complicated by the lack of a negotiating advisor who could speak for and protect the company during negotiations.

The number one rule is don't go it alone. After all, you don't fill our own cavity, do you? You go to a dentist and scream for Novocain like the rest of the civilized world. Why would you enter into negotiations without an experienced negotiator on your side?

Selling your business is not the time or place to learn a new skill. Hire an experienced lawyer, business broker or other agent who can go to bat for you and get the most money possible on the sale of your business.

An advisor or negotiator generally represents the seller of a business and tries to find and bring a qualified buyer to the seller. In exchange, the broker receives a commission on the sale, usually around 3-5% of the selling price (although in some more high-profile cases, 10% fees are not uncommon), plus monthly installments by you, the seller, to help pay some of the upfront expenses related to marketing your business. This fee varies and is based on the size of the company being sold and the marketing to be performed.

The retainer fee may be credited against the commission paid to the broker during the sales process. The broker's commission is paid only when your business goes bye-bye. The commission may be a percentage of the total sale price or a set fee. Often, there is a minimum fee regardless of the selling price.

WHAT YOUR BROKER CAN DO FOR YOU

The services performed by your advisor go beyond dragging prospective buyers by their lower lips to your office and extracting a big, fat check from them. A broker wears a lot of hats.

He or she is a combination accounting, public relations and marketing specialist, although most brokers don't give legal accounting advice. Your broker may put together a business valuation, an asset appraisal, a marketing package and a confidentiality agreement; he or she will also screen prospective buyers, give tours of your facilities and even represent you in negotiations.

A listing of business brokers can be found on the International Business Brokers Association's Web site (**www.ibba.com**).

The business valuation, perhaps the most important document during a sale, may be provided by your advisor or by someone he or she brings aboard for whom preparing these is a specialty. While education, professional affiliations and credentials are not mandatory in the business valuation field, your agent shouldn't be shopping for candidates at the racetrack or the local Laundromat.

Above all, experience should be the most important consideration when hiring a business evaluator. Additionally, if your company assets are a large percentage of the sales price, you may find an asset appraisal is a valuable investment. The business evaluator can help there are well.

A broker also earns his or her money by pulling together a comprehensive marketing package to best display your business to prospective buyers. As the big cheese, you should always review and approve the presentation before it is distributed. A single typo in a marketing package can cast a shadow over your company's credibility.

True story: One financial software company's press release claimed the company was gaining market share fast, reaching "critical ass" in one year. Of course, they could always change the company's mission to making canned chili instead, but the idea is to eliminate those minute mistakes before the public – and potential buyers – see them.

A confidentiality or nondisclosure agreement, which your broker can help you prepare, is an important document you should ask all suitable prospects to sign. It assures the prospect will not talk to your employees, suppliers, customers or their favorite bartender about the sale until an appropriate time. It is very important prospective buyers do not disclose any information about your business to others, except to seek the advice of their counsel, who also must not disclose any sensitive information about your business (and all your business information should be considered sensitive, even the quality and selection of the lunch menus kept in your desk).

Your business brokers will screen prospective buyers to make sure only buyers with the requisite skills to run your company and the financial ability to purchase it are considered.

I knew a guy who worked on a trading desk for the late, great Kidder Peabody Inc., a prominent Wall Street brokerage firm that was bought out by General Electric in 1986.

Nobody can beat GE at building refrigerators or making clock radios, but their ability to trade securities was questioned by many at the brokerage house. In one of the most famous quotes in Wall Street history, one Kidder trader, upon hearing the news that GE had tapped an engineer to run the brokerage, said, "Great, just what we need … a good tool-and-die man."

Needless to say, 70-year-old Kidder Peabody went under within five years. The GE-Kidder match wasn't made in heaven, and a good business broker can ensure that a potential suitor matches up well with you and can keep your business around for a long time.

Your business broker can also be expected to act like a real estate broker and show your "house." Facility tours are generally arranged and conducted by the broker. He or she will answer questions about your business from potential buyers and generally showcase your business in its best possible light.

Your broker may handle negotiations. If so, keep in mind that although the broker generally represents just you, the seller, he or she has a vested interest in completing the sale and will work toward that end.

IS FRANCHISING AN OPTION?

Franchising is one alternative for expanding a successful business.

Franchises are generally of two varieties: The franchisee purchases the rights to a single location or buys a master franchise to develop an area (that is, multiple locations, which may then be sub-franchised, within a given geographic territory). When a business is franchised, a contractual relationship (joint venture) is set up between the successful established business (the franchisor) and the hopeful buyer (the franchisee).

This contract is based on key elements of the original concept that are necessary to duplicate the success of the original business in any number of new locations. The contract will often include a sublease on a location, any changes you want to make to the building's exterior, a complete package of leaseholder improvements, a furniture and fixtures assortment (all with logos and trademarks), an initial inventory package, an initial training package and an ongoing support system comprised of accounting, promotion and general expertise in all aspects of the business's management.

In return for providing this turnkey, proven success package, the franchisor requires an initial franchise fee and will expect to enjoy the daily profits of the business by means of a royalty (normally, anywhere from 2% of the gross sales revenue to 10% of the net sales, depending on the nature of the business and the degree of involvement required of the franchisor).

It is also not uncommon for franchisors to expect from 3-5% of a franchisee's revenues to be contributed to a companywide advertising and promotion budget to promote the business concept and corporate identity. In theory, the franchisee owns his or her business, but in practice, the franchise contract generally removes most creative freedom from the operation of that business.

109

* * *

Ask E-Diva

Dear E-Diva,

I want to start a business, but I don't have the time to put into a start-up business. I have seen many franchises that look interesting. Where do I begin my investigation into the franchise I selected? Please start me out, Diva.

Mrs. Interested in a Franchise

Dear Mrs. Franchise,

There are many organizations you can hire to research for you. However, you will still have to do some work on your own. Franchising is an extensive subject.

First, let's pretend I would be interested in franchising my company. There are at least 7 things you would need to consider:

- ***Capital.*** *As a franchisor, I may require a budget of $300,000 or more to reach expansion goals. This cost is for marketing, printing, audits, and personnel.*
- ***Market trends and conditions.*** *Is the potential franchisee's area a place where my services can grow long term?*
- ***Credibility.*** *Is my company worthy of a franchise?*
- ***Affordability.*** *A new location for a multi-million dollar company may cost $100,000 to start (franchise fee and one year of overhead fees are included in this number).*
- ***Transfer of knowledge.*** *Do I have process and procedural manuals in place to teach a potential franchisor?*
- ***Return on investment.*** *The franchise investment can be measured against other investments of comparable risk that compete for the franchisee's dollars placed in the investment.*
- ***Strength of management.*** *The most important piece of the franchise is its track record in the areas of sales, ad management, training and multi-unit sustainability over time.*

I researched franchising a business because in general they have been proven systems. The advantages to the franchisor are:

- ***Branding.*** *Name of company has some recognition.*

- **Advertising.** *Franchisees usually contribute to common advertising and promotion.*
- **Performance.** *Gross sales performance has been proven.*
- **Speed of growth.** *Has been tested; should only advance in growth.*
- **Limited contingent liability.** *The franchisor does not sign leases.*
- **Return on investment.** *With limited investment, Return on investment will be higher.*

Now this is my two cents; you need to check the following if you don't hire an attorney or a company like **www.ifranchise.net:**

- **www.entrepreneur.com**
- **www.blackenterprise.com**
- **www.franchise.org**

Make sure you do a study on the franchisor's offering and investigate them, along with the, franchisor's experience. The reason you are buying the franchise is to receive the training and on-going support for the business; make sure you ask questions if you don't understand the disclosures.

Here are three more areas that are important:

- **Litigation History.** *Check for any violations of franchise laws, unfair or deceptive practices or convictions of the executive officers. All this gives you information on the creditability of the people and the franchise including the lawyer, accountant, and bank that are involved in the franchise.*
- **Bankruptcy.** *Whether or not the franchise can provide the financial deliverables that are promised to the franchisee*
- **Termination and renewal clause.** *Most franchises have a clause for termination if the franchise does not meet your performance standards or if the franchise is terminated for some reason. The renewal clauses in most agreements are usually set at 15-20 years. The franchisor may renew or decline renewing the franchise agreement. Sometimes the franchisor may request a raise of royalty payments or impose new sales restrictions, depending on the territory or what the franchise board of directors may decides.*

Know how much you can invest and that this is the type of business you can make a return on your investment. Business should be FUN, and you need systems that make work smarter, not harder.

E-Diva

* * *

111

While you can lean on a skilled broker to navigate much of the rocky terrain that covers the sales process, you're going to have to roll up your sleeves and pitch in as much as you can. If you neglect your duties as the owner, you could find the price you get for your beloved business will leave you feeling as flat as the cheap champagne you'll have to buy for your post-sales celebration.

Here's a closer look at the areas of the sales process you'll need to know about.

Business valuation: During a business acquisition, both buyer and seller are concerned with price. Each party needs to determine what they feel the value of the company is. Every business is unique, so setting a price for one is something of an art.

If a business is overvalued, the business will not sell, and if it is undervalued, you may not receive the price you should.

There are three basic approaches to assessing the value of a business: Value based on earnings, value based on assets, and value based on an industry comparison. An analyst may use one or all these approaches, depending on what is appropriate for your company, then conclude with an opinion based on his or her findings and experience in the market.

You have final say about what price to ask for, but again, if it is overpriced, the business will not sell.

According Sanli, Pastore & Hill, a Los Angeles business acquisitions consulting group, determining the value of a business is one of the most complicated and most crucial tasks.

"The question 'how much is your business worth?' is often asked in times of transition and great uncertainty," says Sanli's web site. "The decisions taken on the valuation can have serious consequences."

Sanli says a business valuation is needed when:

- A partner or shareholder wishes to buy out other partners or shareholders.
- An individual or a business contemplates a merger, sale or acquisition.
- Litigated matters such as shareholder disputes, divorce or breach of contract require expert witness testimony on business valuation issues.
- Estate and gift taxes must be determined upon the death of a shareholder or owner of a business or upon gifting of an interest to family or friends.

Consult a business broker or business acquisitions attorney for more detailed information on valuing your business. The above methods are only a snapshot of the basic financial formulas you can use to price your business.

Valuation is more art than science. Your ability to negotiate for a more favorable valuation and terms will ultimately depend on your strategy, market niche, the degree of competition, management strength, entrepreneurial vision, leadership skills and other factors that attract investors and lenders.

Qualifying a buyer: Most serious prospective buyers have specific investment criteria in mind that fit with their skills, lifestyle and personal goals.

The generalist, who looks at every business opportunity on the market, is performing an exercise in self-discovery at your expense. Each agreement is prepared by your legal counsel before he or she is provided with proprietary information. Then your agent should provide you with the prospect's personal financial statement and a resume to show he or she has the means to buy the business and the ability to operate it successfully.

Seller's documentation: As a business seller, you must provide the following documentation to your broker so he or she can successfully represent your business (again, all this information should be held in the strictest confidence):

- Financial statements for the last three years, including income statements and balance sheets (your company must be audited or be capable of being audited for its most recent two years of operations).
- Sales projections for the current year, plus two additional years.
- Aging of accounts receivable.
- Explanation of nonrecurring expenses.
- Tax returns for the last three years, if applicable.
- If the business owns substantial assets in the form of land, property, equipment, stocks and other investments, include any recent appraisals or other relevant information on them.
- Information relative to any outstanding or pending legal disputes
- Leases. If any business property is leased or rented, a current copy of the lease is required.
- Contracts and agreements. A current copy of all contracts is required, as they may have to be renegotiated (it is possible that no renegotiation will be required if a company's stock is sold).
- List of assets (furniture, fixtures and equipment). This list is provided to help with the valuation and is provided to prospective buyers. The depreciation schedule –another list calculating the value of your furniture and fixtures, and so on, over time – is a good source of this data.
- Inventory value. This is the value, or cost, of your current inventory. Compiling this list will give you a good idea of what's laying around your warehouse or inventory storage area, making it a bit easier to clear out obsolete inventory.
- Owner's job description. This is desirable to show the duties of the owner. It will give the broker or advisor an additional tool with which to pre-qualify prospects.

Agreeing on a final price is a delicate process. Be prepared to bargain, and don't be surprised if initial offers are below expectations or contain terms that are simply unacceptable. If you think you're being low-balled, don't get into a snit. It is better to respond with a reasonable counteroffer rather than letting emotions get the best of you.

When you do get an offer you can live with, make sure you get an attorney and an accountant to review all the documents.

113

EXPAND OR DIE

Every company, whether it is a mom-and-pop or an IBM, is concerned about growth. Companies never stand still for very long, especially young, energetic ones. It's expand or expire, with every little room in between.

Consequently, a major portion of an entrepreneur's time is devoted to planning activities that hopefully lead to their company's growth.

Buying a company is only one of several options for expanding a business. However, the way you expand is also partly determined by what aspect of the business you want to grow, which is another crucial decision.

According to Jeff Jones, a business broker and appraiser for the past 20 years and president of Certified Appraisers Inc. in Houston, Texas, business owners have three main choices for what direction their company can grow: Expand in your existing market by getting a share of new business growth; expand into new product and service lines that are compatible with existing lines or expand into new geographic markets.

"All the methods of growth require planning, time and resources that include people, inventory, equipment and money," says Jones. "Because most small to mid-sized businesses have limited resources, if the wrong decisions are made in the attempts to grow, the results can be disastrous."

ACQUIRING MINDS

Expanding through acquisition is one of the fastest ways to grow, and it has been a method frequently used by large closely-held and publicly-held companies.

For many of the same reasons large companies buy existing businesses, small to mid-sized companies can often benefit from this practice.

"Perhaps the best reason is to provide synergy to your existing business," says Jones. "Due to synergism of the combined resources of both companies, sales and profits can often be increased. Sales increase due to the combined marketing efforts, and costs can often be reduced as a result of greater purchasing power, combined facilities and additional skilled employees."

The acquisition of existing businesses in new geographic markets also enables companies to expand into new markets by leapfrogging two to five years over start-up operations. Most companies find it easier to expand from an existing base of business rather than to build from scratch, especially in geographic markets that are not as familiar as the home market.

If you want to roll out a new product line, buying another company may be the best and fastest way to do so. Opening up related lines of products that can be sold to existing customers of the acquiring company can lead to sales growth without adding significant overhead costs.

By way of acquisition, a company can obtain new product or service lines within its existing geographic markets. This works especially well if your company has available space, can obtain new products and services not otherwise available to your customers and has the staff, time and ability to handle the additional lines.

Here are some other tried-and-true reasons to buy and existing business:

- You can review a company's existing track record as reflected in profit-and-loss statements, tax returns, and other financial records, which can all be very helpful in determining expansion plans. Growth potential can be measured based on actual experience rather than the conjecture associated with start-up ventures.

- The need for additional working capital is reduced due to the immediate cash flow being generated by the acquired company.

- The opportunity to gain skilled employees who are familiar with the business operation and market is a major benefit of any acquisition.

- Gaining established customers significantly reduces the time it would take to attract an adequate number of customers to support the overhead of a new operation.

- Obtaining existing licenses and permits can often reduce the time and cost of completing applications, gathering information and conforming to required regulations.

- Sources of capital to purchase existing businesses are more readily available than for start-up ventures. It is very common for the owner of an acquired business to finance part of the purchase price. Banks and other financial institutions prefer to lend money for existing operations that have a proven track records.

LOOKING FOR THE BELLE OF THE BALL

Finding profitable businesses for sale at reasonable prices can be done, it just takes patience, stamina and preparation. Knowing where to look for companies that might be for sale also helps.

Each week hundreds of businesses are advertised in local newspapers, *The Wall Street Journal*, trade publications and their accompanying Web sites. By regularly checking these, it may be possible to find a business that meets your criteria; however, owners are often reluctant to openly advertise their businesses for sale, so other methods may need to be employed.

Suppliers may be good sources of information regarding businesses for sale within the industries they serve. If you call or write to your suppliers and vendors and make them aware of your acquisition criteria, several prospective sellers may surface that are not actively on the market, but would consider selling.

Using direct mail or a direct mail software program or database to contact business owners whose businesses meet your general acquisition criteria can generate potential seller prospects. This method is frequently used by business owners who desire to sell. A shortcoming of this method is you are contacting owners who may not be actively willing to sell, and therefore their motivation to sell may not be very strong, which often results in unacceptable prices and terms of sale.

Business brokers usually represent sellers, and as such they can be a valuable resource of businesses for sale. Their full-time job is to contact business owners and find those who are motivated to sell.

Brokers usually help business owners looking to buy determine a reasonable value for a business, and can often assist in finding financial resources for the acquisition. Business brokers will have knowledge of a variety of businesses for sale, and can help eliminate those for which the price does not make any economic sense.

The broker's fee is typically paid by the seller based on the market price of the business; it is not added to the market price. However, there are a growing number of business brokers who represent only buyers, and for a fee will actively search out the businesses that meet your acquisition criteria. If there is an immediate need to make an acquisition, hiring a broker to do a comprehensive search will produce the quickest results.

Searching the Internet is perhaps the best method for finding businesses for sale. A keyword search will turn up more than 2,000 websites indicating a listing of businesses for sale, like Entrepreneur magazine's Business Resale Network (**www.br-network.com**).

Many business brokers have also set up their own home pages and provide lists of businesses for sale at their Web sites. Some of these sites are national and international in scope. One such site is Bizquest (**www.bizquest.com**), on which more than 100,000 brokers and buyers provide information on businesses for sale. Many local business brokers also have their own Web sites.

Growth through acquisition is a proven way both to get into business and to make it grow. In the past, finding profitable businesses and getting them financed were major problems. Today there are excellent resources to assist in an acquisition search and plentiful sources of debt and equity capital.

Public and large private companies frequently use the acquisition method of growth, and now many small to mid-sized companies are finding it is often less expensive and more profitable to buy an existing business rather than to start from scratch.

Like I said, selling your business, or even expanding it through an acquisition, are tough tasks. But they are tasks that can most definitely be accomplished, ideally to your advantage.

E-Diva
Dr. Rae Pearson

Chapter Ten
Mistakes You Don't Have to Make

" So watch yourself about complaining. What you're supposed to do when you don't like a thing is change it. If you can't change it, change the way you think about it."
— *Maya Angelou, quoting her grandmother*

A lot of my friends in business wish they could invent a time machine.

Whenever I ask them what they would have done differently, I get a wish list as long as a child's letter to Santa Claus.

GOING FOR IT

Two artist business partners I know in New York own one of the hippest cosmetic companies in the industry. They started the business after holding a conceptual art show with a piece using nail polish that caught the eye of the public.

Over coffee once, they reminisced about how fast the business grew and how they wished they had that time back so they could do some things differently.

Just three weeks after the art show, a contact called about traveling and getting their artistic message across to the cosmetics industry. This contact also mentioned they knew some guys who were looking to invest money into a new business idea.

The idea of commercializing their art struck a chord with the duo, who overcame some early doubts about compromising their artistic integrity. They decided to go for it by launching their own line of nail polish and other cosmetics (backed financially by their investors, of course). Within months the two had developed a full nail polish product line.

The business' name also got a lot of attention because it was similar to a Broadway play. Their friends constantly kidded them about it, but these friends stopped joking when the ladies' products were carried by Bloomingdale's and Nordstrom.

Despite this success, other distribution outlets came around with greater difficulty. One particularly high-end spa refused to see their products and on a visit my friend said "Gee, I guess you don't want to see something new." That caught their attention. After the staff looked at the polish they flipped out and said they wanted it in their catalog within 48 hours.

Sounds like they hit it big, right?

Think again.

It takes a long time to translate what you visualize as a business into reality. These two didn't have a lot of business experience, and things happened so fast they got caught up in the whole experience without thinking every decision through.

Outside interference and bad advice were the chief barriers to the company's growth (and to personal fulfillment with business). My friends told me when getting into retail (or any business for that matter) to beware of false prophets.

You are going to find a lot of people (investors, distributors, vendors) who promise you a lot of things. At the end of the day, if those promises don't materialize, then it's you as the owner of the company who's left to make amends.

VOICES OF EXPERIENCE

They say you can't go home again (and you certainly can't go back in time and start over). Still, others' experiences can teach you important lessons.

If you prefer your lessons the easy way (who doesn't sometimes?), peruse the list of tips and wise warnings below, which have been pulled from the experiences of successful entrepreneurs.

The list covers a wide range of issues, such as checking credit ratings of vendors, hiring an attorney, applying for trademarks and patents, getting insurance, creating and using Web sites to sell, tracking the effectiveness of advertising, hiring a consultant, spotting billing scams, leasing offices space, staying healthy and much more.

CHECK OUT YOUR CUSTOMERS

Before signing contracts with new clients or vendors, it helps to have some insight on their creditworthiness.

Do they pay on time or deliver as scheduled? Visit Dun & Bradstreet (D&B) online for answers. Connect online directly at **www.dnb.com**, or through the AOL WorkPlace, which provides business information on thousands of companies **(www.D&B@AOL.com)**, to access your choice of reports on a given company.

D&B's cornerstone product, the Business Information Report ($109), usually includes a company summary, its D&B rating, operation performance, payment patterns, company news, recent financial history and an overview of the company's history. If you need a few key vendors on whom your business will depend, these reports can take some of the guesswork out of choosing the best ones.

For high-risk credit decisions, D & B offers a Comprehensive Insight Plus Report ($149), which adds to the features of the Business Information Report with forecasts of future creditworthiness, an indicator of a company's likelihood to experience financial distress over the next year, an indicator of a company's likelihood to make delinquent payments over the next year, financial condition comparisons to similar businesses, the top 25 domestic and international corporate family relationships, and an outline of key risk indicators.

Another resource, the Credit eValuator Report ($29.99), provides an at-a-glance snapshot of a company's credit information. It does not include a business's background or history.

The reports, which are updated daily or as needed, may also be ordered by phone; call D&B at (877) 753-1441.

BANK ON IT

Wondering if your neighborhood bank is friendly to small businesses like yours? You can find out in *Small Business Lending in the United States*.

This annual Small Business Administration report ranks the lending performances of more than 9,300 banks by state and identifies the ones that are small-business friendly. It's an easy-to-use tool for locating loan sources in your community, the complete report may be accessed via the Internet at **www.sba.gov**.

HOOK UP WITH A LEGAL EAGLE

When it comes to starting your own business, Uncle Sam will be right there – prodding, poking, and bothering you for money and with all sorts of regulations. The government increasingly affects every aspect of small business operation, from relationships with landlords, customers and suppliers to dealings with government agencies over taxes, licenses and zoning.

The best way to ensure you've got everything covered is to hire an attorney with small-business expertise who can give you advice in these key areas

- **Business structure:** Should you form a sole proprietorship, partnership, corporation or limited liability company? Do you know the advantages and limitations of each?
- **Written documents:** Does your lease state who pays for utilities, maintenance and repairs? Do you have an option to renew? Can you sublet? Your leases and other written documents (purchase agreements and employment contracts) should be drafted in clear, precise language and spell out each party's expectations and responsibilities.
- **Co-ownership agreements:** What happens if your partner wants out of the business? Do you have a buy-sell agreement to purchase his or her interests? Does it contain a "non-compete" clause so he or she can't open up a similar business down the block?
- **Licenses and ordinances:** Does your industry require you to be bonded or insured? Will you need professional or product liability insurance?
- **Employee relations:** If you hire independent contractors, do you know how to clas-

119

sify them so you're not penalized by the IRS? Have you prepared an employee hand-book outlining your firm's policies and procedures? What about trade secrets you want to protect?

- **Future planning:** Have you drafted a will or trust to protect your business assets and your firm's continuity in the event you die or become disabled? As a business owner, you should also have a will.

Having a lawyer at your disposal doesn't mean calling on him or her every 15 minutes for counsel. It's not practical, economical or even necessary to contact a lawyer about every business decision you make that could have legal ramifications. Handle the most routine matters on your own.

For example, if you plan to run a home-based business, you can check zoning laws and land-use restrictions on your own to ensure your business complies. If a relative wants security for the money he or she is lending you, simply sign a promissory note, available at most stationary stores.

Another option is signing up for a prepaid legal plan. These services give you access to a set amount of legal services and consultation time for a monthly fee as low as $20.

When you find a lawyer you're comfortable with, follow these steps:

- **Discuss fees.** Once you have found the right lawyer, ask whether he or she charges an hourly rate or a fixed fee. If charges are by the hour, set a cap so you know the maximum you will be spending.

- **Do some legwork.** Keep accurate records, do preliminary research and write out a draft of any agreement you want your attorney to finalize.

- **Use paralegals.** Ask your lawyer about using paralegals for routine legal tasks, like researching public records and drafting documents. Their hourly rate could be half what your attorney charges.

- **Educate yourself.** Special-interest publisher Nolo Press is online at www.nolo.com, or can be reached by phone at (800) 728-3555; or PSI Research/The Oasis Press is at (800) 288-2275. From either, you can obtain a catalog of legal books and software programs for business owners. Also check into legal seminars offered by your chamber of commerce, local business association or university extension service. They can help you learn the basics of legal issues affecting your business.

ONE IS THE LONELIEST NUMBER

Many business owners (me included) start out with a limited budget. This means keeping employee costs to a bare minimum. You may, in fact, only be able to hire one employee. When you only have one person working for you, keeping him or her motivated presents special challenges. Your employee has no one with him to exchange ideas, discuss work problems or share a coffee break. Nor does he or she enjoy the momentum that working with others can bring.

The good news: One doesn't have to be the loneliest number — not if you make a concerted effort to keep your solo employee energized and happy. Here are some tips to do that:

- **Ask for input.** When employees are asked for their ideas and opinions, they will feel vital and involved (and you will have a highly motivated employee). Make sure to tell your employee if you end up using his or her advice, and why. The next time you ask for an opinion, your employee will be more eager to give it.
- **Be accommodating.** When you rely on one employee, you may begin to feel that you can't go a day, or an hour, without that person. Remember to make special allowances, such as giving him or her time off to attend classes or take a child to a doctor's appointment. Always try to be flexible.
- **Set the tone.** Establish ground rules from the start so your employee knows how much authority or responsibility he or she has and clearly understands your expectations.
- **Always reward achievement.** When your employee has an idea that helps you sell to a fussy client or resolve a vendor problem, give him or her praise and thanks (maybe even financial rewards). Before long, your employee will become your strongest ally.

MAKE YOUR (TRADE) MARK

Trademarks and patents can be vital to protect your ideas and your business. It can take a while to gain that kind of protection, but once you do, it's worth it.

I know of a person who planted their ideas in a garden business and has had fruitful results. He was a bartender and bar manager for several years when he came up with the idea for a new plant watering system.

Because he lives in Arizona, top watering his plants was not doing the job. His business plan notes top watering plants is inefficient, as you never know exactly where the water is going. It usually ends up running right down the side of the pot to collect in the drip pan (or evaporates).

Monthly, he had to move a 6-foot-tall plant into the bathtub for a good soaking. One time when he picked up the plant to move it, he rammed it against the ceiling and broke the top off.

This moment of frustration set a light bulb off in his head.

Trying to solve his problem of how to water a plant effectively without having to move it, he dug a little hole in the dirt and poured water into it. It kind of worked. With some more scheming and devising, he ended up buying a syrup bottle, cutting the top off, poking holes in it, and burying it upside down in the plant.

What do you know? It worked!

While the idea seemed so simple and obvious, he still decided to apply for a patent. After going to one of the largest firms in Arizona (and after a $1,000 patent search), he was told the idea probably was not patentable, but that he probably wouldn't be infringing on anyone else's.

Not very encouraging.

He got a second opinion on the patent, and now he is sitting on no fewer than four patents, two of which are amazingly strong. The watering system is selling so well it's all he can do to keep up with demand.

Because he has proven it sells, dozens of new (big name) accounts are slated for this spring, including RiteAid Pharmacy, QVC and the Home Shopping Network. The product has also made a splash on the international market with distribution in Australia, Canada, and the United Kingdom.

How did this root watering system grow so big?

The owner always looked out for number one by protecting his product at all costs through patents and trademarks.

There are people out there who will want to steal your ideas. That may mean getting a registered trademark to help protect your unique product or name from unscrupulous interlopers, charlatans and other corporate creatures of the night.

A trademark includes any word, name, symbol or device, or any combination, used to distinguish the goods of one manufacturer or seller from the goods of others. A trademark should be used to protect a new product or logo before you bring it to the marketplace.

122

A patent can be more abstract and is most often used to protect an idea or invention. Using trademarks in combination with patents can give your product a substantial market advantage.

Registering a trademark with the U.S. Patent & Trademark Offices costs only $275 – far less than getting a patent. The cost for either can rise to $1,000 or more if you use an attorney, though it shouldn't be more than that for a small company.

Patents and trademarks can last as long as you want, as long as you are deemed patent- or trademark-worthy. Some are only for three years or so, and some are for 20 years.

For more information on trademarks, check out the following resources:

- The U.S Patent & Trademark Office, (800) 786-9199 or **www.uspto.gov**.
- Trademark search, **http://tess2.uspto.gov/**.
- Government Liaison Services Inc., (800) 642-6564 or **www.trademarkinfo.com**.

* * *

Ask E-Diva

Dear E-Diva,

My husband and I have a business, and after 20 years I still don't know what the difference is between trademarks and copyrights. How do a copyright and trademark differ?

I hope this is not a stupid question.

Mrs. Can't Ask My Husband

Dear Mrs. Can't Ask,

This is a great question. I used to think they were one and the same, but they are not.

For example, the copyright laws do not protect the names, titles or short phrases; this is where trademark laws protect. Trademark laws protect the product or service name and any slogan used in the advertising.

Copyright is a form of protection provided by the laws of the United States (title 17, U.S. Code) to the authors of "original works of authorship," including literary, dramatic, musical, artistic, and certain other intellectual works.

This protection is available to both published and unpublished works. Section 106 of the 1976 Copyright Act generally gives the owner of copyright the exclusive right to do and to authorize others to do the following:

- *Reproduce the work in copies or recordings*
- *Prepare derivative works based upon the work*
- *Distribute copies or recordings of the work to the public by sale or other transfer of ownership, or by rental, lease, or lending*
- *Perform the work publicly, in the case of literary, musical, dramatic, and choreographic works, pantomimes, and motion pictures and other audiovisual works*
- *Display the copyrighted work publicly, in the case of literary, musical, dramatic, and choreographic works, pantomimes, and pictorial, graphic, or sculptural works, including the individual images of a motion picture or other audiovisual work*
- *In the case of sound recordings, to perform the work publicly by means of a digital audio transmission*

A trademark is a word, phrase, symbol or design, or a combination of words, phrases, symbols or designs that identifies and distinguishes the source of the goods of one party from those of others. A service mark is the same as a trademark, except that it identifies and distinguishes the source of a service rather than a product. Throughout this booklet, the terms "trademark" and "mark" refer to both trademarks and service marks.

And patents are a separate issue yet. While trademarks and copyrights protect product names, artistic or literary work, patents protect inventions.

To register a trademark with the U.S. Patent and Trademark Office or to look at a list of frequently asked questions, visit www.tmcenter.com online.

Also, make sure you hire a good trademark attorney to do the research, and if you file for protection, file federally and in your state. Some people think it's debatable to file so extensively, however I believe in being safe not sorry.

This is an expensive process if you file for federal coverage, and the process can take up to a year before the confirmation is officially received.

Remember, good things take time.

E-Diva

* * *

BE IN GOOD HANDS

One of the biggest mistakes a new business owner can make is to take a pass on insurance, specifically personal disability insurance. Since many young business owners start out with nobody else committed to or knowledgeable about the business, protecting your business investment against personal illness or injury is a top priority.

If you were injured or suddenly became seriously ill tomorrow, could you afford to keep your business running for six, eight or 12 months until you were able to return to work? That means paying your rent, utilities and other ongoing expenses and hiring someone to work temporarily in your place. And could you meet your personal obligations: Home mortgage, car payments, grocery bills and other family needs?

Unfortunately, disability insurance is at the bottom of most business owner's to-do lists. Take my advice: Bump it to the top.

There are three types of disability coverage:

- Income replacement coverage, which replaces income you've lost due to an injury or illness.

- Business overheard expense coverage, which pays ongoing business expenses while you're unable to work. This includes rent, phone, utilities, employee salaries and other costs of running a business.

- If you have a partner, you'll want to consider the third type of disability coverage: Buyout protection. If you are disabled for an extended period of time, it provides the money for your partner to purchase your interest in the business.

Premiums for your disability insurance policy depend on the type of coverage you want, your age and the level of risk an insurance company assigns to your business or industry. Other considerations are whether you want to protect yourself in the event you can't perform any type of work, the length of time you'll wait before receiving payments (the longer you wait, the lower your premiums), and how long the contract will run – for one year or until your retire.

For information about what type of disability insurance might be right for you, consult your insurance agent. Also check with your local chamber of commerce, trade organization or small business association to find out if any of them offer disability coverage to members.

WEB SITES MADE EASY

Building the perfect Web site for your emerging business needn't be an onerous task. Remember, it's an important gateway into your business; it's a place where you can establish a vivid public identity and make a powerful marketing pitch for your company.

125

I'd recommend being as creative as you can without losing sight of the goal that you're out to sell a product.

One Web designer I have consulted with cautions against trying to become the Mardi Gras of the Internet. Too many bells and whistles can drown out your company's message. Your top concern is that your site is compatible with the software your customers are using.

How many people really have that supercomputer needed to handle the multimedia tribute to Britney Spears you've always wanted to add to your site?

To create the right site, start by charting the demographics of your potential visitors. Are they women or men? What ages? What types of businesses do they operate? What are their income levels? How often do they upgrade their computers?

Glean these things from trade association Web sites, by setting up a test site to gather information or by mailing questionnaires to your customers. Using this information, a Web site designer or consultant can match your site to your customers' sophistication level.

Think simple. Most non-technical companies should keep their sites low-tech.

So who gets to use all the fun stuff? Computer-related companies, mostly. More important for most entrepreneurs are the three hallmarks of a good site: Attractive, simple graphics; coherent organization; and presentation and value-added content. Only after those basics are in place should you consider adding high-tech extras.

Here are some more pointers to help you build a great web presence:

- **Choose a name for your Web site carefully.** The name of your site is extremely important. Stick with names that are easy to remember and spell (not supercalafragalicousexpealadocious.com).

- **Chat it up.** Enter online chat rooms frequently, and aim to get in on discussions where you can offer advice in your field of expertise. To build strong relationships that can pay off down the line, strive for one-on-one interactions with Web users.

- **Content is queen.** Keep in mind that better content makes for a better Web site. Never compromise on the quality of your content – that's what draws people in.

- **Take it easy.** One of the most common mistakes people make when marketing online is to use techniques that come across as pushy. The Internet is a medium where members appreciate a delicate touch.

- **Keep promising something new.** Your Web site should constantly promote what's coming up in the near future so users will return again and again. Keep adding to and updating content to improve your site from the day you launch it.

- **Offer to provide content to others.** Electronic newsletters and magazines are always in need of new information. One of the best ways to create an online presence is to e-mail sites and volunteer content on a regular basis.

- **Respond rapidly.** If people visiting your site have questions, reply within a day or two, or you're liable to lose them as customers. Fast response is the single most important factor in retaining Web users.

- **Keep it simple.** When interacting with people online, brevity is the rule. Learn to express yourself concisely so you don't waste people's time.

- **Be patient.** It's unlikely you'll achieve the results you want online right away. Try not to be turned off when people don't respond immediately; follow up several times with potential prospects.

- **Link with like-minded sites.** The more gateways to other sites you have the better. Try to find free links, or "trade-outs" where you offer a link to another business' site and that company provides one in return. It's possible to offer hundreds of links, but make sure they all appeal to your target audience.

- **Be consistent.** Don't expect results if you market your business online only occasionally or haphazardly. Maintain a constant presence so you'll build a solid reputation in the online universe.

- **Market your Web site in other media.** If you advertise in print media, write columns for industry publications or engage in public speaking events, be sure to always mention your website.

WEB CYBER SALES: IF YOU SELL IT, THEY WILL COME

If you plan to sell your wares on the Web (and who doesn't these days?), you can use your Web site as a consumer cyber-center as well as place ads on other well-traveled websites.

If you plan on selling on the Internet, here are a few points to keep in mind:

- **Read Internet newsletters.** The Internet is an evolving environment. To keep abreast of new developments and stay current on new Web sites aimed at their target customers, some business owners read dozens of free online newsletters. Try looking for newsletters that target webmasters or discuss e-commerce or Web site promotion. One such newsletter, **www.virtualpromote.com**, gives advice and alerts readers to the many shady offers for Web business assistance prevalent on the Internet.

- **Be patient and work hard.** Your early months on the Internet may yield little fruit. Remember, people aren't going to just magically appear at your site. Links with other sites are often needed to draw them. I know time is precious for an entrepreneur, but try to spend a few hours per week reading online newsletters and looking for and establishing links with other sites aimed at your target market. Expect it to take about six months to start getting your site mentioned in stories, chat rooms and newsletters with links to your site. It may take nine months or more of networking before you reach what's regarded as the magic number for a successful Web site: 1,000 hits per day.

- **Link with sites that target your audience.** Links allow an Internet business to avoid paying for costly advertising, which may or may not get results, and the best sites to link with are those that already target your desired customer. Young entrepreneurs who sell vintage automobiles, for example, would want to establish links with car aficionado Web sites and any other sites that affluent males between 30 and 60 years old visit frequently. Once you find sites aimed at your target market, contact the owners about the possibility of adding links to your site. When doing this, be careful only to establish links with legitimate sites that provide a benefit to their visitors. Most sites want to know how many visitors your site gets per day before establishing a link. Once you reach the magic number of 1,000 hits per day, major sites are more willing to link with your site (this boosts your site traffic tremendously).

- **Give something away.** Free stuff is always a draw. A young entrepreneur selling children's educational software could provide a few samples that people could download for free. This won't cost the entrepreneur much, if anything, and it helps get the company's name out to the target market. It's also a huge traffic-builder at linked sites, which can mention that free kid's software is available.

- **Find an Internet service provider (ISP) focused on Internet business.** Internet businesses need three important features from their ISPs: The ability to download at least 25 gigabytes of data per month; accurate tallies of the numbers of hits, visitors and link transfers; and a very low percentage (less than 0.5 percent) of downtime during peak business hours. Most ISPs can't provide this level of service, so check with your provider before building your site. You might have to switch several times before finding the one that works for you.

* * *

Ask E-Diva

Dear E-Diva,

I work in a business and we are considering a wireless network environment for our offices. Should we have any other tech thing for our computers for faster computer service? What do you know about this type of stuff?

Ms. Clueless About Information Technology

Dear Ms. Clueless,

Believe me, you are not the only person who feels baffled while searching for answers when it comes to technology questions. I have researched wireless versus digital subscriber lines (DSL) versus dial-up, and boy, is it confusing!

What's best? We recently had a lot of thunderstorms and /lightning, and our computers clicked into frenzy mode.

The DSL stopped running and all the computers had no ability to receive e-mails. The dial-up kicked in instead, and for one week, it seemed like we went backwards.

To make a long story short, after a week of craziness, the DSL was back in place and it made sense to have the redundancy of DSL and wireless or dial-up.

So, which way to go?

Wireless may be a good choice because:

- *Wireless enables employees to move from office to office with laptop computers, hand-held computers or cell phones and not struggle with the network connectivity.*
- *Wireless enables lots of out-in-the-field connectivity to the office.*
- *It requires less wiring in new or old buildings, and keeps the expenses down.*
- *Wireless is not as venerable as DSL or dial-up.*

What I found is that wireless is here, and the most progressive companies are not fighting the wave.

I personally have a wireless PDA (personal digital assistant) and a wireless home environ-ment, and I love it in both places. However, as I mentioned, we have DSL and dial-up in our office. From what I've experienced, it's important to have two systems.

E-Diva

* * *

TRACKING THE WILD AD CAMPAIGN

Advertising is an expensive marketing tool. How can you tell whether it's working?

It's important to monitor the effectiveness of your ad campaigns and to verify that every one of your precious dollars is being put to good use. Try to determine which ad medium is most effective and what kinds of ads perform the best. This reduces waste and helps you plan your future advertising efforts as efficiently as possible.

To help track your advertising results, get interactive with your audience. For example, your ad could ask respondents to call or write for a free booklet. Then track responses by building devices (such as numbered codes) into your marketing materials that help you identify where your respondents are coming from, or even what specific ad on what day they are responding to.

You can track print advertising responses by using a special telephone number or exten-sion, or have mail-in responses go to a specific mailbox. If you have the same ad in three different magazines, give each one a different code that respondents must enter to re-ceive the free material.

You have to get creative and do as much follow-up as possible. You can have the most carefully designed and best executed ad campaign in the world, but it will fail if you don't provide the necessary follow-up.

I recommend entering all the response data into a good contact management database so that even after you've closed the sale, you can maintain contact with your customers by mail or phone on an ongoing basis. Some companies that track ads plug respondents' information into their computer with a coded symbol so they become a part of the company mailing list.

A CONSULTANT, A CONSULTANT, MY KINGDOM FOR A CONSULTANT!

Even Mafia dons have consigliores, so why not hire a consultant?

Sometimes consultants get a bad rap in business media for overcharging (and under-pro-ducing), but consultants often don't get the credit they deserve. A good consultant can provide an objective evaluation of your business, identify problem areas and recommend strategies for solving them.

Plus, consultants offer plenty of flexibility, no matter what your business or what your needs, from accounting, management and marketing to improving your writing or customer-relations skills. If you can get good advice without having to pay a salary, that sounds like a good deal to me.

When you weigh it against the cost of a full-time employee's salary and benefits, the expert advice of an independent consultant can be a worthwhile bargain. Here's what to look for when deciding on a consultant:

- **Understand a consultant's role.** A consultant is an advisor, not a magician. If your marketing campaign hasn't increased sales for the past six months, don't expect a consultant to turn business around overnight. If someone promises to do so, be skeptical. You want a consultant who is knowledgeable in your industry or field, and can offer a workable long-term solution, not a quick fix.

- **Identify your needs.** Determine what you want to accomplish, quantify it into specific goals and write it down. A consultant can't read your mind, and the more specific your goals, the more specific your results. Not pleased with the results of your marketing campaign? Tell your consultant exactly what you want to accomplish; don't just say that you want to create more sales, for example, but that you want to increase sales by 10% or more this year in three target markets and to create a more unified brand identity.

- **Know what you'll commit.** Provide your consultant with whatever resources you can to help him or her do the job. Consider background materials on your business plus any office equipment, space, supplies or employees you can make available.

- **Establish fees up front.** Some consultants charge flat rates or bill by the hour, the day or the project. Others charge a contingency fee where the amount paid is based on results. For instance, if a consultant reduces your operating expenses by $10,000, he or she might receive 10% of the savings as the total fee or as a bonus in addition to a flat rate. The average full-time consultant charges $95 to $150 per hour. Some charge much less. Just remember: You get what you pay for.

- **Develop a list of questions.** Interview several prospective consultants before you make a final decision. Find out what experience they have in your industry, if they've handled similar problems, and if they can give you full confidentiality and represent you without conflict of interest with their other clients.

- **Check references.** Ask a prospective consultant for three recent references (and call them!). Find out if the consultant accomplished what was promised, if he or she communicated regularly and if the company would hire the consultant again. Letters of recommendation are nice, but they don't always tell the whole story. Ask for the names of past clients who run businesses similar to yours.

- **Put it in writing.** A handshake just won't do. Make sure your written agreement spells out clearly the services to be performed, the starting and ending dates, the fee and how it will be paid, expenses you agree to pay and services you will provide. If you have an attorney, ask him or her to review and approve the agreement.

130

For more information on hiring a consultant, check out these resources:

- The Institute of Management Consultants maintains a free referral service for certified management consultants who've completed the institute's professional accreditation program, completed the institute's exam, signed a code of ethics agreement and undergone a screening process. Their site is at **http://www.imcusa.org**, or call at (800) 221-2557.

- The Association of Management Consulting Firms provides a free referral service, categorized by industry and specialty, to help businesses of all sizes select consulting firms. Call (212) 551-7887 or visit **www.amcf.org**.

- You can also find consultants through trade associations in a particular industry. The American Society of Association Executives (ASAE), online at **http://www.asaecenter.org**, can refer you to these trade groups. Write to the ASAE at 15175 I St. NW, Washington, DC 20005; or call (202) 371-0940.

- The Service Corps of Retired Executives (SCORE) is an organization of some 12,400 retired business owners and executives that provides free consulting for small businesses. Call (800) 634-0245 or visit **www.score.org**.

- Small business development centers (SBDCs) are one-stop shops set up by the Small Business Administration to give entrepreneurs free or low-cost advice, training and technical assistance. There are more than 50 centers, at least one in each state and territory. Call (800) U-ASK-SBA or visit **www.sbaonline.sba.gov**.

A POCKET FULL OF (PART-TIME) MIRACLES

Need extra help for just a few months? Having trouble getting everything taken care of in the office, but don't want to fork over big bucks for a full-timer?

One friend of mine hired her father to provide advice and keep an eye on the budget. This employee didn't ask for a lot of money, and who doesn't like getting to tell their parents what to do for a change?

There are several creative ways to get more help without breaking the bank. For instance, bring an intern onboard, such as a high school or college student who works for little or no pay in exchange for valuable work experience. You'll need to make some time to train them, and then keep a close eye on their work, but you can't beat the price.

Draw up a detailed description of your internship, then promote it at the career placement center at your local high school or college. The National Society for Experiential Education in Mount Royal, New Jersey, provides information on starting internship programs on the web at **http://www.nsee.org**, or call (856) 423-3427.

Or get someone with loads of experience and lots of time on their hands. What is Grandpa doing? Senior citizens can bring a wealth of real world expertise to the job, and though retired, many are eager to keep their hands busy in the business world. Check with senior centers in your community and your local branch of the American Association of Retired People (AARP).

If you need individuals with targeted skills, like a graphic designer or annual report writer, freelance contractors might be just the solution. If your business relies on skilled work, consider starting your own work apprentice program. That'll help you mix practical classroom instruction with a year or more of on-the-job training. You'll be working with entry-level talent you can train and eventually hire full time as your business grows.

Job for the Future, online at http://www.jff.org, is a Boston-based organization that's geared toward helping entrepreneurs to establish successful job-training programs. For help or advice, call them at (617) 728-4446.

SCAM ALERT!

It happens all too often: You get a bill in the mail for services or equipment you're not sure you ordered. It seems wrong, but then again the bill has all your correct information, it's not that much money, and you don't have time to chase down all the supporting paperwork – so you just pay it, falling for one of the oldest tricks in the book.

It's relatively easy for con artists to get your vital business information off the Internet or through your competitors and begin invoicing you for fabricated services. Amazingly, many charlatans who engage in this practice get away with it.

Shady characters and unscrupulous snake oil salesmen run a number of scams geared at separating business owners from their money. To help you protect your business, here's quick peek at five common scams and how to avoid them:

Scam #1: Office supply rip-offs. Sometimes the offer sounds too good to be true (and it probably is!). Dishonest peddlers lure their victims with claims of a liquidation sale or a shipment mistakenly labeled with your company's name that you can have at a greatly discounted price.

Other con artists might claim to be conducting an office equipment survey. After you innocently provide information about your copy machine, for example, the individual will call back and pose as your new supplier or authorized dealer for the products you use for your copy machine. You'll place an order, pay them the money and never see a part.

The solution: Whenever possible, do business with local suppliers. Try to do business with people you know in the community. You should also make it a rule never to buy from a supplier by phone or mail before you check out the company's background and references. Insist on written purchase orders; don't accept cash on delivery shipments and don't pay cash for a shipment.

Scam #2: Phony invoices. Knowing small businesses don't use elaborate accounting systems, scam artists often use phony invoices to great advantage.

Here's how it works: The swindler calls your company to get your name and other information. Then he or she sends an invoice for an amount just small enough not to attract attention. The invoice might be for goods you never ordered or for advertisements in bogus publications.

The solution: Set up a system of checks and balances to weed out bogus bills. Every order should be given a shop number. When an invoice is received, pay it only if it has a matching shop number.

Scam #3: Sneaky solicitations. We all get a lot of junk mail, but when I get what appears to be a bill, I examine it closely. This type of close reading can thwart a popular scam that involves what looks like invoices for directory listings or advertisements but are really solicitations, with this disclaimer in very fine print: "This is a solicitation. You are under no obligation to pay unless you accept this offer." Sending solicitations with such a disclaimer isn't illegal. But many business owners miss the small print and pay anyway.

The solution: If a "bill" arrives by second-class or bulk mail, beware. It's probably a solicitation. When you receive a "bill," match it with a purchase order for the product. If you can't find one, chances are you never ordered the item.

Scam #4: Charity pleas. Want to support your community by donating money to build a home for abused children? It sounds like a great cause, but the charity may not be legitimate. Many companies want to help where they can, but often you just don't have the time to check everybody out as thoroughly as you'd like.

The solution: Be cautious. Some solicitors use names that closely resemble those of well-known organizations. Before you give, check with the local charity registration office of your state attorney general's office and with your Better Business Bureau. Internet tools like Charity Navigator (http://www.charitynavigator.org) can help unmask a scammer's ruse. If a caller offers to send a "runner" to pick up your contribution, pleading that the group needs your money now, hang up the phone. It's a scam.

Scam #5: Technical difficulties. A repair technician might offer you a free inspection of your office equipment to ensure it's in good working order. That's fine, unless the technician surreptitiously damages your otherwise healthy equipment and then performs high-priced work to "fix" it.

The solution: When someone solicits you, ask for references. If you decide to accept the offer, insist your equipment remain at your business while it's being inspected or repaired. If you must send your equipment in for repairs, request that damaged parts be returned. If you suspect foul play, call another technician for a second evaluation, and contact the Better Business Bureau (BBB) if you've been ripped off.

You don't have to be a BBB member to receive its free pamphlets, which cover everything from telemarketing schemes and credit card laundering to tips on charitable giving. Contact your local BBB for information.

If you've been scammed, you can report the incident to the National Fraud Information Center in Washington, D.C., where counselors will help you file your complaint. Call (800) 876-7060 or visit **www.fraud.org**.

LEASE LOGIC

If your business is producing goods, it almost always is producing waste.

Don't let the issue of trash disposal (specifically, who is going to pay for it) come between you and your landlord. Headaches of that nature can be avoided by confronting sensitive areas during lease negotiations. Here are some tips designed to keep both landlord and tenant happy as clams:

- **The overall lease:** A lot of small-business owners don't read the lease and don't understand it. It's your responsibility to understand what you're getting into. Remember, the lease document is the rulebook (whatever is in there, you're stuck with it!). Like any contract, the lease should be reviewed by an attorney. Most attorneys can review a lease in less than an hour, so it's not a big expense, and it's a safety valve for potential problems.

- **Is it a good deal?**: How do you determine whether a lease is a good deal or not? Many leases state a base rent per square foot, but this rate can be misleading. Sometimes it includes space that's not useable, such as corridors and elevators, and this makes it difficult to compare two leases for two different spaces. Instead, look at the total amount to be paid. Sometimes a space that's slightly smaller with a higher price per square foot may work out better for your business because it's more efficiently laid out.

- **Length of the lease:** Many new business owners want a short lease or no lease at all. That way, if the business is unsuccessful, they aren't on the hook for thousands of dollars for space they are no longer using years into the future. However, it may be difficult to get a short lease if you're in a tight housing market. When space is scarce, many landlords won't settle for leases shorter than five years. Short of working out of your garage, the only recourse you have is to move to a part of town where rents are cheaper but where your neighbors may not subscribe to *Martha Stewart Living*.

- **Tenant improvements:** You may manage to save money by making improvements yourself, but most leases require the landlord's permission. Submit your plans before you sign the lease.

- **What's included and what's not:** Too many small business owners focus on dollar amounts without considering what they get for their money. Some tenants pay for utilities and a percentage of common-area maintenance. Many law firms have a gross lease, which includes all expenses, but some tenants sign a triple net lease in which they pay their own property taxes, insurance and maintenance. In such cases, the base, no-frills rent is less. For my money, base rent is a better deal when you're just starting out. Just keep control of the thermostat and wear a sweater in January. Also watch for non-monetary clauses. Will heating and air conditioning be shut off after business hours or on weekends? This may be important if you plan to work odd hours.

- **Subleases and allowable uses:** If you decide to move or find you're using just part of your space, you may want to sublease or assign the lease to another business. Most leases won't allow this without the landlord's approval. Most leases also specify the type of work you can do on the premises. Landlords tend to make this "allowable use" as narrow as possible. In most cases, negotiate to make it broader, to allow for future expansion of you business.

- **Pass-through expenses:** A common trap for tenants is the annual increase in operating costs, or "pass-throughs." Often landlords will ask for a 4-5% annual increase to protect the landlord against inflation. These days, the increase often is more than the inflation rate because the soft real estate market of the early 1990s forced landlords to forgo any rent increases for a long time. Watch for inaccurate calculations of operating costs; overcharging tenants 10-15% is not uncommon.

Before you go out to negotiate that lease, here are some lease terms you should know:

- **Lessor:** Landlord.
- **Lessee:** Tenant.
- **Right of first refusal:** Before vacant space is rented to someone else, landlord must offer it to the current tenant with the same terms that will be offered to the public.
- **Gross lease:** Tenant pays flat monthly amount; landlord pays all operating costs, including property taxes, insurance and utilities.
- **Triple net lease:** Tenant pays base rent, taxes, insurance, repairs and maintenance.
- **Percentage lease:** Tenant pays for base rent, operating expenses and common-area maintenance; landlord also gets a percentage of tenant's gross income (most common for retailers in shopping malls).
- **Sublet:** Tenant rents all or part of space to another business; tenant is still responsible for paying all costs to landlord.
- **Assign lease:** Tenant turns lease over to another business, which assumes payments and obligations under the lease.
- **Anchor tenant:** Major store or supermarket that attracts customers to a shopping center.
- **Exclusivity provision:** Shopping centers can't lease to another tenant who provides the same product or service that existing tenant does.
- **CAM:** Common-area maintenance charges, including property taxes, security, parking lot lighting and maintenance; may not apply to anchor tenants in retail leases.
- **Non-disturbance clause:** Tenant cannot be forced to move or sign a new lease if building or shopping center is sold or undergoes foreclosure.

Once you find a place to put down the roots, here are some questions to ask before signing the lease:

- Does the lease specifically state the square footage of the premises? The total rentable square footage of the building?
- Is the tenant's share of expenses based on the total square footage of the building or the square footage leased by the landlord? Your share may be lower if it's based on the total square footage.
- Do the base year expenses reflect full occupancy or are they adjusted to full occupancy (that is, real estate taxes based on an unfinished building are lower than in subsequent years)?

- Must the landlord provide a detailed list of expenses, prepared by a CPA, to support increases?

- Does the lease clearly give the tenant the right to audit the landlord's books and records?

- If use of the building is interrupted, does the lease define the remedies available to the tenant, such as rent abatement or lease cancellation?

- If the landlord does not meet repair responsibilities, can the tenant make the repairs, after notice to the landlord, and deduct the cost from the rent?

- Is the landlord required to obtain non-disturbance agreements from current and future lenders?

- Does the lease clearly define how disputes will be settled?

QUICK PICKS

You can access dozens of commercial online databases where you can get the full text of important business documents. Here's a sampling:

- **Reference USA (Formerly American Business Disc):** Directory information on over 12 millions U.S. businesses, including address, phone number, sales, number of employees, contact names and more.

- **FedBizOpps (FBO) (Formerly the Commerce Business Daily) (http://cbd.savvy. com):** Full text of announcements issued by the Department of Commerce on contracts, procurements, requests for products, research and service needs of U.S. government agencies.

- **National Trade Data Bank:** Collection of databases produced by the U.S. government on domestic commerce and international trade.

- Lexis/Nexis (**www.lexis-nexis.com**): If you have access to a university or law school library, check this out. This exhaustive online database is divided into two parts. Lexis covers U.S. and state legislation, court cases, bills and legal issues. Nexis provides articles from business newspapers, magazines, periodicals and company annual reports.

FOR FUTURE REFERENCE

Following are the most useful reference books you'll find at your public library:

- *Business Information Desk Reference: Where to Find Answers to Business Questions* (Macmillan): This tells where to find information on almost any business topic, from finding funds to starting a business.

- *Encyclopedia of Associations* (Gale Research): This guide lists thousands of associations for practically every industry imaginable.

- *Encyclopedia of Business Information Sources* (Gale Research): This bibliography has 24,000 citations on 1,100 subjects, listing directories, encyclopedias, yearbooks, online databases, trade groups and professional societies.

- *Gale Directory of Publications and Broadcasting Media* (Gale Research): This is a listing of newspapers, magazines and radio and TV stations by geographic area.
- *Industry Surveys* (Standard & Poor's): These publications cover 69 major domestic industries with prospects for future activity.
- *Thomas Register of American Manufacturers* (Thomas Register): This comprehensive guide lists thousands of product manufacturers.

FINALLY, BE HEALTHY

One of the chief complaints of my entrepreneur friends has to do with time: There isn't enough of it.

Running a business gobbles up every waking moment, leaving you precious little time for yourself, whether to hit the gym for some stress-relieving exercise or to hit the couch for some much-needed downtime. Getting away from the office is harder and harder, but try (I know it's hard) to take as much time for yourself as possible.

A tired worker loses focus, is more uneasy, and stressed out more. You deserve that time, even if you really only wind up stealing away hours, or minutes at a time.

Looking and feeling healthy is easier than you think. All it takes is a little adjustment. So close your laptop, get off your tush and follow these five steps:

- **Walk.** Use coffee breaks at business meetings and conventions to take a brisk stroll (not enough to break into a sweat but enough to loosen your muscles). A 5- to 10-minute walk will raise your heart rate, increase your oxygen intake, burn additional calories and increase your metabolic rate. Your body will feel energized and your mind sharp.
- **Stretch.** Take two or three minutes every hour to stretch your upper body, shoulders and neck. You can do a simple routine while sitting at your desk
- **Avoid sugar.** The sweet rolls and cookies often found at conferences may taste great, but the sugar they contain provides only a short-term energy boost. Sweets act as a natural depressant in the long run.
- **Limit caffeine and alcohol.** Coffee, tea, wine, and alcoholic drinks will dehydrate you and limit your ability to focus.
- **Drink water.** The amount of water you drink each day should equal, in ounces, one-half of your body weight. If you weight 140 pounds, that's 70 ounces, or seven 10-ounce glasses, each day. So take a water bottle with you and fill it (and drink it) regularly.
- **Read a good book.** Like this one! Or watch a good movie.
- **Relax.** And make sure you sleep healthy hours.

THE FOOTPRINTS OF JABEZ AND HIS LITTLE PRAYER

1. To ask for and expect God's blessing for today.

2. To plead for more "territory" and step forward to receive it.

3. To lean precariously but confidently upon the Holy Spirit to guide my thoughts, words, and actions and to work in the supernatural realm to accomplish what I could not.

4. To ask God to keep evil from spoiling the blessing

   He desired to bring about through me.

   REACH BOLDLY FOR THE MIRACLE!

   (The Prayer of Jabez)
   1 Chronicles 4 : 10 (NKJV)

Now, let's start that business or decide on an excellent career for you.

993238